W O R S H I P   M A T T E R S

Truly
Present

Practicing Prayer in the Liturgy

Lisa E. Dahill

Augsburg Fortress

TRULY PRESENT
Practicing Prayer in the Liturgy

Editors: Suzanne Burke, Jessica Hillstrom
Cover and interior design: Laurie Ingram
Cover photo: St. Gregory of Nyssa Episcopal Church, San Francisco, California; © David Sanger Photography

ISBN 0-8066-5147-4

Manufactured in the U.S.A.

09   08   2   3   4   5   6   7   8   9   10

Contents

1
Introduction to Contemplative Prayer and Liturgy

Simon and his partners are exhausted, not to mention frustrated, and ready to call it quits for the day. They've been going since sundown the night before, working hard all night in their boats, and have caught nothing. Now it's morning and they are discouraged, cleaning their nets on the shore. They have families to feed, and it's hard to come home empty-handed after such a long night of effort. The sunrise was beautiful an hour ago—it looks like a lovely morning—but to Simon its beauty is flat, its freshness no joy on a day with only hunger ahead of him. Simon senses a presence, looks up, and sees a stranger watching them. Suddenly he realizes other people are arriving too, and they seem to be gathering around this man. How odd. Soon a crowd has assembled, and the stranger comes over and asks Simon if he would mind rowing out a bit with him so he can address the crowd. He must be some kind of teacher. Simon is curious, and besides, there's no hurry to go home. Better to delay that painful moment when his family sees him coming with empty hands.

The stranger introduces himself—his name is Jesus—and they row out a short distance. Even in his exhaustion, Simon senses that what this man has to say is intriguing. Stories. Parables. His manner is intriguing, too, powerful and authoritative yet completely disarming somehow, as if he speaks out of some reservoir of simplicity that needs no force. His voice, his stories, stir something in Simon—some longing he can't quite name, a glimpse of the beauty and mystery of things in a way he's never sensed before. Who is this guy? When Jesus has finished speaking he turns away from the crowd, faces Simon, and thanks him. Simon is struck by his gaze at such close range: it's as powerful yet disarming as his voice, and looking into his eyes Simon finds the longing suddenly deepening in him. Perhaps Jesus sees something in Simon's face too. For he says, quite gently and unexpectedly, "Put out into the deep water for a catch." Simon's impulsive spirit wants to retort, "There's not a fish anywhere out there, believe me—no way am I going to break my back one more time today with those nets!" But he doesn't want to insult the stranger, and curiosity is welling up in him again. He says simply, "Sir, we have been working all night and have caught nothing. But if you say so, I will let down my nets." Why not, what can it hurt?

He rows out to the deep and lets down his nets, and is stunned to feel them sagging almost immediately under a huge weight of fish. What is going on? He tries to pull them in and quickly realizes it's far too much for him alone, even with Jesus' help. Frantically he waves to his partners James and John to come help, and when they have hauled in the net, nearly breaking it's so full, they can hardly contain all the fish in both boats. In fact, they are about to sink under all this abundance. Simon Peter is overwhelmed with astonishment; this whole experience with Jesus is suddenly too much for him. Jesus' teaching, his gaze, his invitation to let down into the deep, his providing for Simon and his partners and their hungry families with this abundance that shines of God—in a despairing flash Simon is consumed by his unworthiness in the face of such awe, such mercy.

He falls down before Jesus and can hardly speak: "Lord, go away from me, for I am a sinful man."

In the silence following his words Simon can hear the waves lapping up against the boat. He can't bear to look at Jesus for fear of rebuke, Jesus' face once so kind surely now angry to see how unworthy Simon has proven to be. Clearly Jesus thought he was entering the boat of a righteous man able to welcome him and all his gifts, rather than the boat of such a sinner as himself. The silence isn't long in real time, though it feels like an eternity to Simon. But when Jesus speaks again, by some wonder his voice is even more gentle than before. It's redolent with mercy, of a sort Simon has never heard in his life unless perhaps in that moment his mother first received him newborn into her arms, a mercy so strong it seems to actually enact what it speaks: "Do not be afraid." In the love borne in those words, that voice, Simon finds himself lifting his gaze, raising his head, so that he is looking with awe straight into Jesus' astonishing eyes when Jesus says, next, "From now on you will be catching people." And when they had brought their boats to shore, he left everything and followed him (Luke 5:1-11).

What does this story stir in you? Did you notice some movement of your own heart as you read this narration of the call of Simon Peter and the first disciples? For instance, perhaps you could relate to Simon's discouragement at the end of a fruitless night of work. Or perhaps you felt something as Jesus got into Simon's boat—a desire to welcome Jesus into your boat too? Or an unexpected aversion to his coming so close? Perhaps you wanted to spend more time listening to Jesus teaching the crowds. What might he be saying? Your heart strains to hear. Or perhaps you responded to Jesus' gaze or his invitation to Simon into deep waters, to let down his nets there. What stirs in you at these invitations? Do you sense a longing and curiosity like Simon's, or some other response altogether? And the miraculous catch of fish—perhaps your heart swelled in awe at God providing for Simon's family's need. Perhaps Simon's feelings of unworthiness echoed in you, or the wonder of Jesus' easing his fear. Perhaps you found yourself riveted by Simon's transformation and new vocation, or his leaving everything to follow Jesus.

Wherever you found yourself "in" this story, whatever moved in you as you read it or heard it, is an invitation into prayer. You can stay in the story, wherever you are, and bring your feelings and reactions, your desires and fears and needs and resistance, right into prayer, talking to Jesus just like Simon did and learning to listen for his response to you. Living into this story of encounter with Jesus and hearing your own call from him can be a life-changing and ongoing experience, as Simon-who-became-Peter discovered. People spend their entire lives learning their way into this story, on ever deeper levels. Yet it is a story accessible also to those who, like Simon himself at the story's outset, are strangers to Jesus. In this way the story in Luke 5 is a window into the church and especially its worship. Worship is a gift never exhausted, always fresh and new and endlessly transcendent even to those who have been Christians all their lives, yet welcoming in just the ways they need even of those new to the faith.

In worship each Sunday we arrive, like Simon Peter, in the midst of our work weeks, our ordinary lives, and encounter Jesus—often in ways we are not expecting. In worship we too are invited to let Jesus into our boats, and to listen as he speaks to us. In worship we hear Jesus inviting us into deeper waters, to let down our nets even in our "dark night" periods that feel as fruitless and hopeless as Simon's. In worship we experience the abundance of God poured out beyond measure to fill our hearts' and bodies' hungers, breaking the nets we try to contain it in, filling our boats and drawing us in awe to our knees. In worship we confess our inadequacies and hear Jesus' reassurance of love. And in worship we are astonished to discover new vocation emerging, to return to the world with lives made new, perhaps transformed as radically as Simon Peter's and his friends'.

This book attempts to open up that invitation deeper into living encounter with Jesus Christ in and through all we experience in worship. Many Christians, even lifelong worshipers, struggle at times to engage more deeply with the mystery we celebrate each Lord's day. We may wonder if there is more to the faith than we are experiencing. Some even leave their congregations or denominations, or the Christian church entirely, convinced that these inherited rituals and hymns are a far cry from "real" spirituality which by definition must be found elsewhere. And indeed it does at times appear as if other traditions—Buddhist meditation, Catholic monasticism, Hindu ashrams—do a more effective job of inviting people into those depths of contemplative experience of which so many people, indeed our whole loud, glitzy, consumerist culture, seem endlessly needy. Yet in fact we don't have to leave our tradition in order to experience God in new, radical, and life-changing ways. We don't have to leave our churches or our real lives in order to enter the story of Luke 5. What we often do need, however, is *help* in learning how to move to this deeper level of spiritual experience at the heart of the Christian tradition. That heart is found in worship. And the help we need in moving into the heart of the tradition, the heart of worship, the heart of God, is found in practices of contemplative prayer. This book is written to introduce you to a series of contemplative practices rooted in the core traditions of Christian worship, intended to help you learn over time both to worship more fully and to let worship encompass ever more of your "normal" life, at home, at church, and in the world.

So what is contemplative prayer? For that matter, what is spirituality? We hear these terms thrown around, and indeed *spirituality* is used to mean nearly anything, at times in ways contrary or downright hostile to Christianity itself. People use the language of "spirituality" to imply escape from the messy, conflicted worlds of community and public life, work and family, the nuts and bolts of ordinary human life. *Spiritual* can seem to mean disembodied, ethereal, other-worldly, or highly individualistic. Persons who consider themselves "spiritual but not religious" make clear that their spirituality is something quite other than the rituals, practices, sacred texts, and graced/flawed communities of faith called the church.

Yet, despite its problematic usage in many circles, in reality the term *spirituality* is an inherently Christian term with a rich history. Rooted in New Testament usage, the word *spiritual* refers to any person or reality animated by the Spirit—and not just any spirit but the Holy Spirit of God in Jesus Christ. A graceful and Spirit-filled life, a life rich in the fruit of the Spirit, a community transparent to the living reality of Jesus Christ alive and incarnate—these are *spiritualiter* (Latin); this is authentic *spirituality*. The term *spirituality* arose in the early centuries of Christian existence, referring not to transcending the constraints of religion but to being embraced and formed by the Spirit of God in Jesus Christ. And of course the Spirit animating Jesus—and us through and in him—is anything but otherworldly, anything but privatistic, anything but disembodied or isolated from others. Thus when we speak of truly *Christian* spirituality we are reclaiming this original understanding of what it means to be spiritual: openness to the creative and redeeming presence of God in Jesus Christ, through the Holy Spirit. This is Spirit-ual. This is Spirit-uality. And this is the spirituality people long for right here in our churches: the Spirit and presence of Jesus alive in our midst, in our hearts, in our bodies, in our liturgies, in our world.

What then is contemplative prayer? It is a way of becoming attentive to this Spirit, to Jesus himself in our midst. Prayer is fundamentally a process of learning to attend to God; it is allowing oneself to become aware of the endless *encounter with God* potentially present (at least as far as God's initiative is concerned!) at all times in us. That is, prayer means learning both to arrive with the fullness of our heart, mind, body, feelings, and experience into the living presence of God and to receive the revealed fullness of God's own heart, word, body, love, and reality for us in ever-deepening mutual intimacy. Prayer is speech and silence, listening and speaking, rest and attentiveness.

Prayer is relationship, a love affair: spending time with the Beloved and opening as much of oneself as possible to this fiery radiance of love, this tender incarnate Love our hearts so endlessly desire.

This is not easy. Intimacy is never easy. And so the practices called *contemplative* give assistance in this process, a kind of scaffolding for the encounter with the Beloved. The word *contemplative* derives from a visual metaphor: learning to "see" God, to behold the One who holds and beholds us always. A contemplative then is not some world-denying recluse but, in this root sense of the term, is a person learning to keep the soul's eyes open to the presence of God in all things, at all times, in all dimensions of one's life. Practices of contemplative prayer do just that: they help us, each of us, practice "looking for" God, listening for God, attending to God, becoming devoted attendants—servants—of this One who is mysteriously at work in all things for good.

It is simultaneously the simplest and the most difficult thing on earth to pay attention to God in Jesus Christ. We see a vivid example of this, in all its power and grace and difficulty, in the story from Luke 5. The initiative comes entirely from God. Jesus shows up in Peter's life, unbidden and unexpected, and continues taking the initiative throughout their relationship: from inviting himself into Peter's boat to directing him out to deep waters and into a new vocation. But though the initiative comes entirely from God, like Peter we can choose whether or not to follow. The human dimension of this process is our struggle each new day between the impulses of the "old Adam or Eve"—the sinful self in us that resists God's invitations into love—and the call of Christ. We see our side played out in Peter's role in the story. Peter welcomes Jesus into his boat, listens to his teaching, and obeys when invited into deep water and to let down his nets. So far so good, we may think. This looks easy enough. But when he sees the miraculous catch of fish, and catches a glimpse of the awesome divine power shining through Jesus' words and presence, Peter is overwhelmed. He is unable to remain looking at Jesus and all that Jesus is bringing into his boat, his life. He looks away. To be specific, he looks at his sins. He turns away from the abundance of fish, his own awe, and Jesus' face, and fixates instead on his sin. And watch what happens: as soon as Peter's attention is diverted he says, "Go away from me, Lord." What looks like holy and commendable behavior—a confession of sinfulness before the righteous Savior—turns out here to be deadly, for it drives Peter into a despair that cannot tolerate Jesus' presence any longer. Peter's attention is diverted from Jesus, and he tries to push Jesus away. And Jesus responds with mercy: "Be not afraid."

At this point Peter has a choice. And we know that he did listen. He turned away from letting sin define him, raised his head, and looked into the eyes of the One addressing him with such unexpected mercy. This is discipleship, the life of following Jesus, of listening to him, hearing his call, getting up from all that entangles us, and following. Contemplative practices help us, like Peter, learn to look at Jesus and not be distracted by other realities, such as self-scrutiny and condemnation, or how much better than ourselves others seem to be faring. These practices help us learn to hear Jesus and recognize his voice, to distinguish it from all the other voices tugging at our awareness. They help us learn to stay close to him, abiding in him, letting our hearts live where true joy is found. Most of all, contemplative practices help us worship ever more fully. They invite a certain lingering in word and sacrament, music and prayer, not rushing from one thing to the next. Here, week after week, we are learning to fully *receive*, to surrender to God in the mystery that is worship.

This book is intended to help you learn about contemplative practices that can help you be truly present in worship—and invites you to try them in your own prayer. Each chapter has two parts. The first part of each chapter explores some aspect of the eucharistic liturgy with an eye to its contemplative dimension: how we attend to Jesus' presence *here*. Always the focus is not so much on how worship ought to be conducted, as much as what helps us grow ever more attentive to

God in Jesus Christ through the Holy Spirit—here and now, in worship. The second part of each chapter introduces two prayer practices that help to deepen the sort of prayerful attentiveness to God the chapter is exploring.

Because this book is practice-centered, it will be best used if read over time rather than in one sitting. You might read a chapter each week, alone or with a group, and choose one of the practices in that chapter to try in prayer that week. Most of the practices are intended for daily use and work better in a regularly scheduled prayer time than on the fly, but some (such as spiritual direction) take place less frequently, and others (such as refraining from self-attack) are meant to be practiced throughout one's life. If you are not presently in the habit of daily prayer and weekly worship, simply adopting a rhythm of daily *and* weekly presence to God is itself the most significant practice of all. At least during the period you are reading this book, see if you can find space for ten or twenty minutes of prayer a day using one of these practices each week and for Sunday worship with your congregation. Once you've finished, eight weeks later, you may find you can't imagine living without these daily and weekly immersions in the mercy and reality of God. The Sabbath commandment—like all the commandments—is meant by God to be *gift* to us, not burden. Living in our broken, sin-distorted world and lives, we need regular immersion in the sheer reality of God. I hope in some way this book may encourage your desire for God in both daily prayer and worship.

These are indeed radical forms of prayer: surrendering to God and simultaneously discovering God kneeling at *our* feet, washing us, anointing our wounds, breaking the bread, feeding us with love over and over and over, for all the years it takes—indeed, for a lifetime of grace. The practices described in this book are intended simply to get you started. Some of these prayer forms may already be familiar to you, perhaps so familiar as to seem time-worn, whereas others may seem fascinating or odd. Perhaps you will be drawn to prayer forms that help you experience God in ways that come naturally for you.

Or you may feel invited to experiment with practices that draw you deeper into less-developed parts of your experience. Either way, the purpose is always the same: to let these practices open you ever more fully into the presence of the One who is endlessly attentive to you, to let Jesus into your boat and your heart, and to let his presence begin to encompass ever more of yourself, your time, your world. Don't worry whether you're doing prayer "right"; to abide in the arms of the Beloved is all that matters. Whatever draws you there, and helps you stay there, is all you ever need to do. Ultimately these practices— and this book—are intended to help open connections between your depths and God's, centered in worship and nourished in prayer, to help you learn to live at this level of deep communion with God right in the heart of your life, in the heart of the world.

For reflection, discussion, journaling, or spiritual direction

1. What moved you in the story from Luke 5, particularly with regard to experiencing Jesus?
2. If you do not usually pray to Jesus directly, how does it feel to imagine doing so?
3. When or how often do you usually pray? What helps you attend to God (for example, reading the Bible, meditation, walking, group prayer)? How do you wish you could grow in prayer?
4. Do you have a favorite image or name by which you address God?
5. What does "keeping the Sabbath" mean to you? What do you most long for on your days off?
6. What is the most meaningful worship service you have ever experienced? What made it so?
7. What aspects of worship do you presently sense as most transparent to you of God's presence (for instance, music, preaching, eucharist, passing of peace, prayers, beauty of sanctuary)? Try to be as concrete and specific as possible.
8. Where in this chapter did you sense the Spirit moving in you? Return to that word, sentence, or paragraph and listen for where your heart is being stirred. Bring your feelings, questions, or responses to God in prayer and/or journaling.

2
Gathered and Called by Name

In a widely read 2000 book, *Bowling Alone: The Collapse and Revival of American Community,* sociologist Robert Putnam traces forms and degrees of human connection in the U.S. He shows how, to a startling extent, this nation—whose extensive networks of religious, civic, and other voluntary associations have been one of its key strengths for generations—is becoming a country of loners. Overworked, commuting long distances, far from birthplace and family roots, and turning for solace or recreation increasingly to "virtual" or other solitary or home-based forms of recreation, contemporary Americans enjoy much less of what Putnam calls the "social capital" that formerly knit people of many stations in complex relational connections. Organizations like Rotary or Kiwanis, church circles, hospital or school volunteer pools, neighborhood or issue-oriented political networks, and even bowling leagues are often hard-pressed for members. Clearly this increasing fragmentation of civic bonds hurts our society, providing fewer opportunities for people to connect with each other particularly across barriers of class, race, and culture, and fewer means for meaningful broad-based participation in the direction and life of the institutions that sustain us all.

One might argue, however, that although society doubtless suffers from decreasing forms and "thickness" of social capital, families may benefit given that time and energy once invested in neighborhood, church, or clan are now spent at home. But family life is not in good shape either. Many studies have documented the strains bearing down on U.S. families of all social classes. The number of times the average family eats dinner together each week or minutes the average parent spends each day talking to children, or spouses to one another, bear witness to the increasing fragility of human connection.

These concerns have not diminished since the turn of the twenty-first century. The "cocooning" and "nesting" instincts of the late 1990s, intensified following the attacks of September 11, 2001, may have drawn people home for solace. But they have not resulted in noticeable deepening of the human and relational ties we need to sustain our lives. Even the religious dimension of our lives, that last bastion of solace for the isolated, pressured—but church-going—souls Americans are, appears to be less sustaining than we might hope. In a recent book, *Landscapes of the Soul,* Douglas Porpora reports on a wide-ranging series of interviews with people of all ages cataloging a startling degree of human disorientation: from oneself, from others, from a clear sense of purpose or meaning in life, and from a God seen (even by most of the churchgoers in the interviews) as fundamentally disconnected from one's innermost soul.

Of course not every person who enters your church this coming Sunday is a walking billboard of these concerns. Many of our parishioners—probably more so than "average" Americans—do still volunteer, take time for their children and marriages, and perhaps even go bowling together. Even the fact that they show up on Sunday morning shows that they are aware of their human needs for connection to others, to traditions of hope and meaning, and to God. Nevertheless, even among faithful and active church members, signs of strain appear. People burn out under far too many responsibilities piled into their limited days and hearts, with too little relational juice to sustain them. As they always have, marriages crack open, or children have needs their parents cannot meet; addictions take root, depression or abuse or anxiety haunt even the sturdiest souls among us. Unemployment, serious illness, disability, loss, and grief knock the stuffing out of people, and without adequate familial, social, or intergenerational networks to support them in these crises, they show up on Sunday morning carrying incredible burdens of isolation and pain.

Even those with a strong faith and healthy human bonds may arrive in worship exhausted and depleted in any given week, or simply longing to connect to deeper levels of existence than their ordinary lives allow. How much more those whose connection to God is tenuous at best, or who feel the ache of loneliness acutely? At times people's pain grows so intense they may even contemplate suicide: what use am I really? Does anyone really know or care that I exist? Chances are such persons pass through your pews at least occasionally, and chances are no one around them has any idea of their pain. Member or stranger, child or adult, we all hunger to belong, to be known by name, to be loved and cherished. And God knows this hunger. God greets us—indeed comes running to embrace us—Sunday after Sunday.

Beckoned by God in some way, we come to church. From our very entry into the sanctuary from the busy world and the crowded narthex, we are moving into holy space. Every Sunday or mid-week service represents a threshold moment, an occasion where the usual rules of our daily existence are suspended, new and holy realities may surprise us, and we become open to transformation in the living presence of God. To enter such holy space means crossing some sort of threshold: both literally, as we move through the doors or implicit boundaries of the sanctuary, and metaphorically or symbolically, as our hearts move into increasing attentiveness to the One who is endlessly present to us. We know from studies in anthropology around the world that thresholds are important, marking sacred from profane, inner from outer, safe spaces from dangerous ones. And so our transition into the holy space of worship represents a "threshold moment" as well: we are quite literally entering a new reality. To mark this physical and spiritual transition, this movement enacted as always for Christians in both our bodies and our hearts/souls/spirits, the liturgy provides three interrelated gifts: baptismal remembrance, the sanctuary itself, and greeting in the name of the triune God.

The presence of the baptismal font full of water at the entrance to the church reminds us of our sacramental entry into the body of Christ and invites us to re-claim, re-new, that watershed event this day. Here it is that our true identity is found: child of God, endlessly and personally beloved. Here we are brought into new and irrevocable connection to one another across every human barrier. Here we touch, splash, and trace on our bodies the living sign of our incorporation into Jesus Christ himself, to be physically and fully part of him, breathing his Spirit, bearing his name, marked with his cross and resurrection. Hands and fingers wet, we mark the sign of the cross on our foreheads or bodies as the truest sign there is of who we really are, whose we really are in the face of all doubt or despair: *you belong to Jesus Christ*, whose death embraces your depths and whose rising raises you to God.

Moving into the sanctuary itself, we may bow or genuflect, or stand to pray, before taking our seats. We may kneel in our pews or sit and gradually relax into the presence of this Love that welcomes us and has called us by name. And the space we are in—this space called "sanctuary" from the Latin *sanctus* or "holy"—helps us in this process of arriving into God. The sanctuary helps us as the sensory, sensual creatures we are: visually, aurally, and in tactile and olfactory awareness. The colors and arrangements of flowers, candles, or paraments; the cross, a familiar statue of Jesus, or stained glass windows; the architecture of the space and the ways this building opens our souls to the soaring majesty of God or embraces us in an intimate warmth—these are visual dimensions of the sanctuary's welcome into God. Aurally, people are helped by silence and by prelude music whose style "feels" transcendent and inviting into God. Thus chat and greetings are best left to the narthex. When people come into the sanctuary, they cross that life-giving threshold into God's presence more easily when this space is treated with reverence, a place unique in our demanding, distracting world where people's attention can at last be directed particularly to God.

To cultivate a space where prayer is invited and chat minimized is not somehow inhospitable to visitors or loved ones but a most gracious way of helping welcome them as fully as possible into the Love they long for. This is not to say that visitors should not be greeted warmly and attentively at the door and at the peace, welcomed in prayers, guided helpfully as needed through the service, and made much of in coffee hour or other opportunities for hospitality. Indeed they should! For visitors *and* members, in fact, the quality of a congregation's welcome and life together affects the emotional tone of the sanctuary itself, its capacity to function as *sanctus*, as holy ground. The ways we treat each other at all times need to echo the attentiveness and care with which God meets us in worship—and without this mutual warmth and reverence outside the sanctuary, our coming together within it in God is made more difficult. This is particularly true for children and youth, as well as those who are feeling fragile or needy: the care they receive in other dimensions of the congregation's life has everything to do with how they will perceive the sanctuary, worship itself. People who are ignored or shunned, let alone violated or mistreated by others, will never be able to allow their deepest selves to unfold in that congregation's worship. No matter how beautiful, its sanctuary will not be worthy of the name.

In baptismal remembrance, and in the beauty and reverence and emotional tone of the sanctuary itself, we are invited into the Love that gathers and greets us. And as the service itself commences, we are greeted explicitly, verbally, in some way in the name of God. Whether using the traditional triune formula or not, the pastor's liturgical greeting claims the assembly, this assembly, into the desire and reality of God. The apostolic greeting in both *Lutheran Book of Worship* and the Renewing Worship liturgies of Holy Communion use trinitarian language and images from the New Testament: "The grace of our Lord Jesus Christ, the love of God, and the communion of the Holy Spirit be with you all." Echoed by the assembly ("And also with you"), this greeting grounds the entire proceedings, our communion here in this place, in the prior initiative of this triune Love embracing each person gathered. What a difference this makes for all that is to come! The liturgical greeting makes explicit the One whose love is the only real point of our assembly and alone makes it possible, the true host of this gathering. Without this sort of greeting we fail at the true hospitality people are starving for, that for which they chose worship today over the golf course or the shopping mall: the invitation into the living presence of this very Lord and God.

In these three elements—baptismal remembrance, entrance into the sanctuary, and pastoral greeting in the triune name—we see key ways the church invites people into the living presence of God in Jesus Christ. Tired and lonely, stretched thin by the demands of our lives, perhaps doubting our lives' worth or God's passionate love—even the very reality of God—we arrive at church longing for just the sorts of immersion into God in the human body of Christ that this threshold-crossing initiates. These gathering elements move us out of the world of noise and chaos, destruction and desolation, need and confusion, and into a world—still created and tangible, indeed highly sensory and human—embraced in the beauty of God, a world of profound personal love and a community of reverence and warmth. Here we are known and cherished, claimed by name at our intimate depths by the One who created all things, who brings us together with these finite companions to journey together in love of God and obedience to God's call in the world.

But how can these practices of gathering carry over into the rest of the week? Let me suggest two ways.

Prayer practices

Baptismal remembrance

First, we can take up Martin Luther's own practice of letting baptismal remembrance be a daily gift, not just a weekly one (let alone occurring only at confirmation, once in our lives!). We can do this personally, splashing ourselves with water first thing in the morning or at the end of each day, making the sign of the cross, letting go of the failures or stresses of the previous day as we return to our true identity: beloved of God. We can also practice this daily return to reality with those who share our homes, our families, or friends. At day's beginning or end, at departures or returning home, we can trace the cross of Jesus on one another's foreheads and remind each other quite tangibly of the love that holds us all together. In time, such "crossing" of one another becomes an indispensable part of each day, a way of enacting God's divine welcome, our true home, day in and day out.

Part of what helps us return to our primal baptismal identity in Jesus Christ is simply to spend time with him each day. As in church, so in our own homes we need sanctuary spaces, places of beauty or silence or contemplative music, spaces to hear the living Word and nurture healing relations. Alone and together, we need sanctuary for our hearts in God. Families today struggle to find time even to eat together, but with some initiative meals can also include time for prayer, resurrecting the early Lutheran practice of home devotions. Many resources for family prayers exist that can help. Even—or especially—with the busy schedules so many of us struggle with, we need sanctuary time personally as well. Twenty minutes alone, resting in the arms and mercy of God, perhaps a candle lit before an icon, can make all the difference. Later in this book we will look at many forms of prayer that can help you move deeper into that mercy of God, but in order to begin, simply the existence of sanctuary space and time in your life is essential: it incarnates God's desire for you and your own freedom to take time for God.

Refraining from self-attack
Second, just as the congregation's sanctuary cannot function as such—cannot readily invite people deeper over time into the presence of God—if the emotional tone of the congregation is cold or abusive, so too in your heart's sanctuary. Your heart's opening into the radiant and healing presence of God will shut down every single time, without fail, if you greet each tiny opening of feeling or need or sin or desire in yourself with self-attack. Contrary to what may have been drilled into you early in life, in truth God does not delight in condemning you. The condemning voice inside you is not the voice of God; even if its words sound pious, its tone makes it by definition a demonic invader. Over and over in the gospels we see Jesus refusing to condemn or withdraw from sinful or unclean (i.e., "disgusting"-seeming) people of all kinds, the insane and demonically possessed, needy and demanding and childish people—indeed, children themselves. Not only does he not condemn them or push them away, in fact, he actively seeks them out and desires to draw close to them. The only people he ever berates are—surprise—those religious leaders who condemn. By analogy, the aspect of your humanity most distant from Jesus is *not* your sin or failure itself, the weakness you hate in yourself, the shame or desire or poverty or need you may find so abhorrent at your core. It's the "righteous" voice in you condemning yourself (or others)! Jesus longs to embrace all of you, especially those places most shadowy and hidden, most in need of his light and love. He certainly won't leave your sins in charge, your shame unloved, your needs unmet; don't worry. But you will never be able to bring them to him at all as long as you are shriveling yourself with attack.

So a key practice of fundamental importance for all the forms of contemplative prayer in this book is to learn Jesus' own tenderness toward the *sinful, unclean, hated, weak, or childish places in yourself.* Refrain from self-attack, even in everyday internal chatter ("I'm such an idiot…," etc.). Guard your tongue from snide or rude comments directed toward others in that same voice. And particularly in prayer, as you move into your own sanctuary space, let Jesus be your guide. If you can't bear to face some feeling or aspect of yourself surfacing in God's presence, let Jesus receive it … and watch how his tenderness greets your greedy self as he greeted Zacchaeus, your insane rages as he received the Gerasene man possessed by demons, your childish needs as the disruptive little ones he embraced.

For reflection, discussion, journaling, or spiritual direction

1. What is your heart's primary need right now? Can you express that to God? To others?

2. What does your baptism mean to you? Do you or your family practice any daily re-connecting to God?

3. What in your congregation's worship space helps welcome you into God's presence? Visually, aurally, with other senses, or emotionally—what do you love about worshiping there?

4. Where else in your life do you feel welcomed into God's presence? Is there a place in your home or elsewhere that feels like a "sanctuary" to you?

5. What aspects of your daily or ordinary reality do you need to step out of in order to enter the sanctuary of God's living presence? What helps you make this transition?

6. How do you react to the suggestion of refraining from self-attack as an ongoing spiritual practice? Do you have other internal habits that block your prayer, your capacity to receive God's love, or your capacity to share it?

7. Where in this chapter did you sense the Spirit moving in you? Return to that word, sentence, or paragraph and listen for where your heart is being stirred. Bring your feelings, questions, or responses to God in prayer and/or journaling.

3
Confessing the Texture of Our Lives

In worship we enter consciously into the presence of the One who loves us more passionately than we can imagine. We move across various thresholds: through the door of the sanctuary, through the baptismal waters, and deeper into the presence of love. We might think that, brought out of the chaos of our worlds and invited endlessly close forever into this love, we would gratefully, gracefully relax into God's arms and let this reality of love claim us completely. And at times we do: those rare moments when somehow the doors open and we cross not only the church's threshold but that deep internal one at the heart of each of us as well, and allow our whole being to be washed and clothed and embraced in Christ.

But at other times we resist. We may come through the church's doors. We may trace Jesus' cross on our bodies with baptismal water and go through the motions of prayer. But somehow we find ourselves unable to cross that internal threshold as easily as the external one; somehow the inner doors remain closed. We get bored or distracted in worship and nothing seems to reach us. Maybe we think the children are too loud, or the hymns are lame, or the sermon goes on too long—there's always something to complain about. Perhaps the prayers and lessons remind us of some aspect of our lives we would rather not think about. Why come at all? On some level, made obvious when we choose to stay home from worship but present often even when we're there, we resist God. And this resistance to God plays out throughout our lives.

We resist God. We resist accepting this love into which we are so freely and eagerly invited, this healing our souls and relationships and planet so desperately need. Despite our best intentions it's easy to forget God and live in ways that deny the divine image in ourselves and others. Whether on Sunday in church or the rest of the week in our prayer and relationships and vocation, we may claim to be Christian and want to be Christian yet some part of ourselves clings to that inner threshold for dear life, kicking and screaming and refusing to let ourselves be dragged in to love. And God, who will never coerce, does not force us.

Why do we resist God? Why aren't we running as fast as we can to the One whose presence promises healing, consolation, and joy? Why, given the weekly availability of manna and mercy through word and sacrament, the heavens opened, the fountains welling up, would we ever hold back, let alone stay away altogether? Why resist God? Because we're human, because we're sinners, and because we're aware at the most realistic part of ourselves that letting go into God will cost us everything. This manna is utterly, entirely free; but it is not cheap. We resist—we choose to starve in the presence of abundance—because accepting God's love at the very core of ourselves will change us entirely. It's about conversion, turning, a new heart. It's about transformation, putting on Christ, dying to our old selves and being reborn entirely in him. This sounds good in theory, but in reality it's terrifying. We resist.

Although this resistance is normal and universal, it is not the end of the story. Because we are baptized, we are saints as well as sinners. We have put on Christ already; joined to his death and resurrection we are freed of our former helplessness in the face of sin. The church's practice of confession, part of our baptismal immersion into Christ, helps us. We all need help in this area. And the help we need is personal, at times uncomfortably so. The safe, anonymous practice of general confession in worship, using prayers pre-printed in bulletin or worship book, is inadequate as a sole vehicle for this process. This is the case for two reasons. First, such confessions provide some of us the comforting illusion that despite whatever we may have done or failed to do in our life this week, now God forgives us and no change is necessary. Lutherans know our salvation is entirely by grace anyway. Great! So I can return to my life and go on as before, and next week I'll come back to church and be "forgiven" again. This is what Dietrich Bonhoeffer calls "cheap grace," and it is poison to Christian life. Of course grace is *free*, but it is far indeed from *cheap*; to expect forgiveness without repentance and the sincere desire and intention to change one's sinful ways is blasphemy.

Relying on general confession can be problematic also in the other direction, too, namely with those who are acutely aware of their need for repentance. Here general prayers can fail us by their inability to pinpoint the *actual* sins at the heart of our lives. One of the real surprises in the spiritual life, if we are lucky to have insightful confessors, is that what we thought were our worst sins often turn out to be ephemeral, and the real problems—the inbred sins that suffocate us and keep our hearts closed to the living mercy of God—turn out to be things of which we were quite unaware. The fact that we know we are sinners does not mean we know our sin. Part of our blindness includes blindness to the real and surprising ways we resist God; for sin's real-life constellations and configurations are as particular as each one of us before God. Thus general confessions can be harmful not only to devotees of cheap grace but also to those who sincerely desire to confess, because often the sins we have in mind, of which our blinded conscience accuses us, are the wrong things. At best, we waste years of our lives confessing symptoms rather than our core woundedness itself. And at worst we confess the wrong sins entirely, beating ourselves up over imagined failings while blind to the ways we truly do resist God's love for us.

Thus the practices of this chapter are intended to nurture a deeper self-awareness before God that will help us grow in real, heart-opening confession. Practices like these help prepare us to confess our true sins when we come together in worship, so that the absolution we receive goes to the heart of our need. Thus these practices do not replace but make possible effective public confession.

But let me note one final thing. Because confession is typically linked with sin, we think of it as depressing, humiliating, having our noses rubbed in our failings. Alcoholics hitting bottom, drug addicts on the streets, families whose problems escalate out of control—these people may be forced to face their sins (and they often report how exhilarating it is to begin finally to tell the truth about their lives and face their real problems). But for most of us, such radical honesty and truth-telling sounds worse than death. Short of total last-resort desperation, we won't go near it. And in fact, it is a form of death: that death into which our baptism has drawn us. It really does require radical stripping of our barriers and defenses, gradual release of the "pleasing" selves and psychic strategies we developed as small children for sheer survival, a nakedness before God and trusted others that can feel more frightening than anything we've experienced in our lives.

So why do it? Why would anyone embark on such a journey? Quite simply: this is the Christian life. It is the very shape of our lives, baptized into Jesus' own death and stripped of all that separates us from God. Of course we can resist this journey—we demonstrate that every day. But fundamentally the reason why we or anyone would desire *not* to resist but to grow as best we can in the love and mercy—and even the death to sin—this journey involves is that this is the way that brings *life*. Resisting our resistance, confessing our sin, letting God open the closed, suffocating parts of ourselves to newness of heart—this is *life* for us! It is indeed difficult; it is the very way of the cross. But Jesus who will never abandon us knows the way, in fact he is the Way. In him the cross we fear at all costs is not dead at all. In him this cross sprouts shoots, leaves, fruit; it becomes the tree of life.

And so this difficult way of self-knowledge and repentance, confession and turning, turns out to be life and joy not only someday beyond death, but—surprise!—all along the way as well. For despite its radical and terrifying vulnerability to the gaze of human others, the practice of confession is also, most fundamentally, a God-centered practice. And for that reason it is a place of extraordinary liberation and grace. Here, with the help of the Holy Spirit and trusted companions along the way, we bring our weakest, most shameful, most shadowy and hidden parts of ourselves into the open.

For many people, these shadowy places include not only sins but also gifts: desires and strengths in ourselves we are afraid of or were early forced to hide. Like the man possessed by demons (Mark 5:1-20), core parts of us may be infested with self-hatred, alienated from reality, wild with terror or rage, and bruising ourselves savagely in our madness. We are horrified with ourselves and imagine God too must look on us with revulsion, all hell breaking loose within us. But watch how tender and bold Jesus is: he shows up and does not despise the demon-possessed man, nor run away, but sees this horrible, insane part of ourselves—and loves us right there. He sees the human being amid the tombs and filth; he casts out our demons and loves us, clothes us, restores us to our right mind and to our life in community with others. He is astonishing. He is softness. And confession is our chance to invite him ever more fully in all his tenderness into ourselves, our raw need. Whatever is within us, no matter how frightening, we open to him and allow our whole selves to come into the daylight of his amazing, unconditional love. We allow ourselves to be seen and loved *just as we are*, with nothing hidden, nothing suppressed, nothing pretended any longer. It's an incredible mercy.

And it's also a tremendous liberation: all that energy put into self-suppression, hiding even from ourselves the parts of our hearts we are afraid of, is now suddenly released. Miracle of miracles, in the gaze of Jesus Christ we are entirely embraced in love and can let go of the masks we use to hide ourselves from God, others, and ourselves. We are free to tell the truth with all boldness—and this truth-telling quickly moves far beyond our sin. Freed of crippling shame, utterly forgiven, released to know and claim our strengths and gifts, we suddenly find that *God* is the truth we passionately want to "tell" in our lives. Facing God, loving God, caught up in God and opened over and over and over to love, we live with increasing freedom as God's own beloved in real life. Far from keeping us somehow obsessed with sin, authentic confession moves inherently into love, into radical freedom against all powers and principalities in the world, and into praise.

Prayer practices

Examen

"Examen of consciousness" (also known as "examination of conscience") is an ancient Christian prayer form most commonly associated with St. Ignatius of Loyola, sixteenth-century founder of the Society of Jesus (Jesuits). It is a practice of daily fifteen-minute prayer, traditionally at night, and its purpose is to reflect on the day now ending, especially on one's experiences, feelings, and sense of God's presence. The practice of examen is intended to allow the Holy Spirit to deepen your awareness of where God is in the various levels of your life: events, relationships, feelings, moods, stirrings, shadows, desires, needs, hopes, all those intimate places where your own self with its utterly unique mystery comes close to the mystery of God for you today. Thus it gives on-the-ground insight into where you are experiencing (and resisting) God in real life. The practice of examen, or a comparable form of daily self-awareness, grounds several of the later practices explored in this book as well.

Note that examen is a form of prayer: conversation, encounter, rest, intimacy with the Beloved, not sterile self-evaluation or condemnation. Its purpose is to bring as much of your day, your raw experience—thus yourself—as possible into the unconditional, personal love of the One who created you and delights in all of who you are, who longs for your life's freedom and growth in love. By doing so, you learn to pay attention to what God is revealing to you in your life's experiences, both inner and outer. You begin to notice concrete instances of things or persons or situations in your life which strengthen or weaken you—which either bring you closer to God and the goodness of your life, giving you energy and joy and peace, *or* leave you feeling dry, confused, anxious, or exhausted. The meaning or implications of these patterns is not necessarily obvious; they are simply important to notice, and to begin to bring into prayer.

The practice of examen moves through five steps. As in many of the practices explored in this book, here too these steps are simply invitations into God's presence. Initially you will probably do best to move through them intentionally, trying to bring ever more of yourself and your feelings to God at each step. Once you start to become familiar with the process, however, you may sense God inviting you to linger in certain places as you pray. At that point, don't worry that you're not "finishing" the prayer—being with God *is* the prayer.

1. *Prayer for enlightenment.* The examen is concerned with gradually growing insight into the mystery of one's life before God. Such insight does not come with moralism or self-punishment, but by the mercy and revelation of God, so begin by praying for this mercy, trusting in God's never-ending desire for your fullness of life. As you begin the practice of examen, relax and breathe in the love of God for you, asking God to fill your prayer.

2. *Thanksgiving.* Examen moves first into gratitude to God for the gifts of this day as you look back on it from within God's love. For what are you grateful in *this* day? Note quirky or fleeting things that may have seemed insignificant at the time

as well as joyful experiences of grace. Name before God not what you think you *should* be grateful for, but what you really *are* thankful for today. What you are actually grateful for may take you by surprise. Certainly our lives look different when viewed from a place of gratitude, awareness of God's deep, intimate, and abiding presence: this is where we begin. Spend time with God savoring these experiences of gratitude. See if God wants to show you more in them.

3. *Survey of consciousness and actions.* Here we survey the day now received in gratitude. Primarily, we ask what has been happening in us, how God has been working in us, what God has been asking us. Often the places of gratitude are the most obvious initial points of awareness of God's presence and action, but there may be other places as well where we were aware of God today. We also look at how our actions have either reflected this awareness of God's presence and movement, or resisted these movements. Where was God at work in you this day? How did you respond to God's movement? What feelings arise as you remember these things?

4. *Prayer.* This step is traditionally called "contrition," but it expands to mean bringing to God *all* the feelings that emerge in remembering the day. This may indeed include contrition, the honest recognition of places in our day where we ignored or resisted the love of God desiring to move in or through us. The purpose of contrition is not shame or despair but the opportunity to return to the One who longs for divine love to be experienced in all fullness in our lives. Its purpose may also include a recognition of our limits, our woundedness or exhaustion or incapacity at times to respond with the freedom or love we might desire. You might notice here for the first time today, for instance, how tired you are and simply be invited to rest in the arms of God. Or your survey of the day may move you to great joy in the gifts of your life. In any case

tell God all your feelings, even the painful ones, as you look back on your day. Note also if there were places you needed God this day but felt only absence. Tell God about that as well.

5. *Hopeful resolution.* The final step of the examen marks our entrusting of the day to God and gazing deeply into the eyes of God for guidance and hope for the day to come. In this process, a desire for how God might be inviting you to live tomorrow may emerge. This resolution flows out of the first four steps and reflects the particular ways in which God has been moving in you in this prayer and in your life as a whole.

Variant: Group examen. Examen can be a wonderful practice as a shared prayer with your spouse, family, or a regular group of friends. Over dinner or at bedtime, or after gathering in silence and prayer, share your responses to these questions, reflecting on this day (or the last week or month since you met):

- What am I most grateful for today (or in this time period)? When did I feel most *alive*? What made this event or situation so special to me? Where do I sense God was in that experience, or what was God like for me there/then?
- What did I most struggle with today (or in this time period)? When did I feel life draining out of me? What made this event or situation so hard for me? Where do I sense God was in that experience, or what was God like for me there/then?

These questions are often enough for lively, nourishing daily conversation with families. For groups meeting less frequently, the following questions can help deepen the reflection:

- What is helping me stay connected and oriented to God in prayer in my life these days?
- What is distracting me from prayer or gets in the way of my life with God these days?
- How can we best support one another in our shared orientation to God?

Variant: Journaling. The practice of examen conducted alone is fruit-fully done as a form of journaling. Here I simply want to mention one aspect of this process, namely writing one's reflection on the day *to* God. That is, instead of, "I felt grateful to God for Kristin," say, "Lord, thank you for the time with Kristin . . . " and continue with whatever that experience opened up in you. This gets harder when you're exploring places in your day you felt resistant to God, or acted in ways you're ashamed of. Like all prayer, journaling requires that you not try to impress God, or spiff up the truth just a bit, or even lie outright. These painful parts of the day may sound unbearably immature or mean-spirited when laid out in all starkness, so even in writing things no one but God will ever see, it can be tempting to elide the truth into more holy-sounding sentiments. Don't do it! God doesn't want your holy sentiments; God really and truly wants *you* just as you are. Tell God outright what you did and felt in the events you're relating, as ridiculous or blameworthy as they may feel to you. And in the process, remember to refrain from self-attack! The point of such journaling is simply to open yourself to the One who loves you beyond all measure and to begin to listen for God's perspective on the events you're re-experiencing. More likely than not, you will find mercy springing forth where you least expect it—toward your-self in all your weakness and need and humanity, and toward those around you.

Spiritual direction

As human beings we are inherently limited, riddled with blind spots that our best efforts will never detect. We need one another's help desperately in learning to tell the truth ever more fully in Christ. For many of us therapeutic help provides crucial insight at some point or another. Regardless of whether a person needs therapy, all Christians—at least all those desiring continuing growth in Christ—need spiritual direction of some kind. Typically this is practiced infor-mally. A primary locus of spiritual guidance is through preaching;

another, through ongoing conversation with friends who hold us accountable to the love and way of Jesus Christ when we lose our orientation to him. The catechumenate at its best includes personalized spiritual guidance for those coming home to Christ, and churches of all stripes have small group ministries intended to shepherd members in Christ on an ongoing basis.

Alongside or in addition to these, however, many people benefit from more formal spiritual direction as well. Here a person meets with a trained director on a regular basis, typically every three or four weeks. In this hour together, the directee is invited to explore where she or he has been experiencing God's presence. We may get in touch with where we have sensed God moving in recent weeks, or experience God's surprising presence within a situation we had thought was devoid of God. This process of attending to God in one's experience can then allow the presence of God to open up in new ways right in the session itself. A similar process can take place in group examen if participants have the sensitivity, maturity, and time to allow sustained vulnerability before God to unfold. When it does, in formal spiritual direction or in groups, the experience of being simultaneously intimate with both God and human other(s) is almost unbearably grace-full. The director, group leader, or other members can help keep a person on track, returning over and over with him or her to God's presence when distractions or resistance flare up, and experienced leaders can help directees learn to distinguish God's voice and presence from those of deceitful spirits. Through the practice of examen as well as spiritual direction of some kind we learn over time, not merely in the abstract but quite concretely, what our perennial pitfalls are, what the voice of Jesus really sounds like, and the ways he is inviting us personally to grow in him in freedom, courage, and love.

For reflection, discussion, journaling, or spiritual direction

1. Recall times you confessed something fearsome to God or another person. What helped you tell the truth? What happened when you did?

2. What sorts of things do you have the most difficulty confessing? Why?

3. Are there people to whom you can tell the truth about your life? Are there people who can tell their truth to you? What gives you courage to say hard things in love?

4. For what in the last twenty-four hours are you most grateful? Where did you most closely sense God present?

5. Do you journal? What do you experience in journaling? How does writing *to* God change how the practice feels for you?

6. Where do you primarily receive spiritual guidance or direction from others? What blocks you from seeking more intentional forms of spiritual direction?

7. Where in this chapter did you sense the Spirit moving in you? Return to that word, sentence, or paragraph and listen for where your heart is being stirred. Bring your feelings, questions, or responses to God in prayer and/or journaling.

4
How Can I Keep from Singing?

In the experience of conversion—confession and divine forgiveness tasted at the very core of ourselves—we are released into praise. Slave trader John Newton was a notoriously foul-hearted creature who in the middle of a terrible storm at sea in 1747 experienced the depth of his need before God and underwent a profound conversion. Finding he could not grow in the Christian life while pursuing his career as a slave trader, he left and eventually went into the Anglican priesthood in England. But he never forgot the marvel of this conversion; all his life he gave praise to a God who could show such astonishing mercy to anyone as hopelessly entangled in sin as himself. His hymn "Amazing grace" describes the wonder of love releasing him from enslavement to sin and hell on many levels. Eventually his writings and preaching on the evils of the slave trade, rooted vividly in his own experience, influenced William Wilberforce to begin the movement that in 1807 (the year Newton died) abolished the slave trade in the British empire, and in 1833 freed all British-owned slaves. Amazing grace indeed! This grace was costly—it cost Newton everything, his entire former way of life—even as it opened him and many others to the pearl of great price.

Newton's praise overflowed into song. He could not keep from singing. And so it is with us. If Jesus Christ really is Lord of heaven and earth—and of me, utterly and entirely, nothing held back—then indeed, how can I keep from singing? (*With One Voice* 781). In music and hymns and all the sung portions of the liturgy we too are invited into the mystery of God transcending words. We sing, "Lord, have mercy," "Glory to God in the highest," "This is the feast, alleluia!" We chant the psalm, entering it together antiphonally or responsively. We sing as we present our gifts at the altar, as we soar into the "Holy, holy, holy" rapture of heaven itself, as we worship the "Lamb of God who takes away the sin of the world." For thousands of years Christians have sung these liturgical songs, our hearts finding here clear orientation, the scaffolding of heaven for lives complex and faithful here on earth. And for five hundred years Lutherans have cultivated traditions of music and nurtured new generations of music-lovers, people who (like many other Protestants) were raised singing. If you were raised in the church, you most likely have memories of favorite hymns or songs you have loved since childhood, or perhaps you remember the comfort of hearing your parents, relatives, and other familiar voices blending around you in worship before you were old enough to follow the words or music yourself. Often music carries our heart's deepest memories at levels beyond verbal access. People with Alzheimer's who may not recognize their children, spouses, or other close companions are often able to join in with "Jesus loves me" or "Silent night," to the amazement of others. Somehow music carries its meanings into the very heart of us and takes abiding root there. Think of the songs you knew in high school; you have fun at reunions with friends from that age entertaining each other with these songs you haven't thought of for twenty years that are still intact within you.

Clearly music has a great power to form us, even at levels of which we are scarcely aware. Luther and other early reformers recognized this and cultivated new traditions of music—sung sacred poetic and scriptural texts—in order that what took root in people's hearts and popped spontaneously into their heads throughout their days might be good and nourishing fare indeed. Most of the classic hymns of the faith are called "classic" for good reason: they are among the relatively few that have proven able to speak to human hearts across generations and in new cultures and situations. "Amazing grace" is a good example. New hymns and musical settings, richest often in cross-cultural contexts, can unquestionably provide a freshness and immediacy that many "old-fashioned" hymns seem to lack, and we would be impoverished indeed if we sang only hymns composed by people now dead. But when you show up for worship the week your spouse is diagnosed with cancer, or your job funding is cut, or your child is shipped off to Iraq or to prison, you are likely to long for the resonance with the pits of human experience and God's endless love a hymn like "O God, our help in ages past," or "Precious Lord, take my hand," can provide, especially if you still hear this hymn in your grandmother's voice, singing it to you over supper preparation.

At those moments, just as in the moments of astonishing radiance of praise, we sense how powerfully hymns and liturgy—music and prayer united—move us into the living love and mercy and presence of God. Even the opening notes of a well-beloved melody can open your heart, and as the congregation moves into actual singing an amazing thing happens. Not only are we joined together in this most human, most intimate, most un-hip activity of common song, but each person is invited to let the words and music of the hymn or liturgy penetrate his or her own inmost being as well. It's an activity, like worship itself, in which the most solitary and most communal dimensions of our experience join in what can open into an exquisite rapture of praise, or the most cathartic lament. When it all comes together—my heart's present need and desire for God, my capacity to sing through tears in communion with these gathered friends or strangers, and the words and music of the hymn or liturgy itself somehow opening up to God's actual living presence—it's no wonder Luther (quoting Augustine) spoke of singing as "praying twice," or prayer twice deepened.

How can we help one another grow in such praise? What factors of performance and language and style and excellence help hymns or songs or liturgical pieces, as they flow together in worship, become transparent to the living reality of *God* in our midst? To be avoided at all costs are two extremes. On the one hand, we obviously want to move beyond *stultifying* music: pieces played as if by robots, chosen without apparent connection to themes or images of the day, and unspooling at the rhythm of turtles or jackrabbits. Here we experience music ground out for no apparent spiritual purpose at all. But at the other extreme, it can be just as deadening spiritually to experience *over-stimulating* liturgy where, in the hopes of keeping people perennially entertained, never even at risk of boredom, we are always doing something new, shifting liturgical settings or offering no liturgy at all, using different prayers and new orderings or movements or songs all the time. The same effect, in somewhat different form, can come in congregations where too much emphasis is placed on excellence of performance, with soloists or choirs replacing congregational singing. Obviously others' performance can move us at the deepest level, but worship is not a show. People need to experience the word sung, resonating in *their* voices and bones and hearts.

For the greatest value of worship, the reason people come to church at all rather than staying home with their TVs, is finally not entertainment. It's, well, *worship*. The reason people come to church is to experience those moments when the liturgy and music and readings and prayers and sacraments and the faces of loved ones—indeed, our own body and life and all the world and cosmos—begin to shine with the glory of God who transcends and pervades all things. We can let go at last, right here in the moment, right here in worship, into adoration and humility and love. Such worship is not fed by unceasing novelty. Nonstop novelty keeps us tied to a bulletin or the projection screen to find out what's happening *now,* what the words to *this* prayer are, etc. Worship, rather, is fed by enough familiarity that we can trust the service itself at some point to carry us and move into real presence. We are able to sink "inside" these prayers, texts, and movements—and let them open up into God—only when we're not constantly on edge, when our attention can rest *entirely* on God and not the mechanics of what's happening next.

We want people's focus, finally, not to be on worship leaders, however excellent, nor the bulletin and what comes next, nor the marvels of some cutting-edge technology, but on God. Not what will immediately impress visitors, but what best helps us *and* them become "lost in wonder, love, and praise" over the long haul: that is our purpose, the real question to consider. Of course the liturgy can seem strange to those new to the faith, but that's true of any religious or social practice of formative depth when viewed from outside; it's no reason to dilute what, once internalized, becomes a precious shared opening to God. Visitors need help learning liturgies and negotiating hymnals, and most congregations can improve significantly in providing such help in warm-hearted, user-friendly ways. But what will keep these visitors coming back again and again is the transcendent awe and adoration and praise of God alive in the midst of worship itself. The untamed, life-transforming power of praise spilling forth from hearts alive to God is riveting and contagious and will draw them back for more. In fact, it will draw them *in*, to continue their journeys loved and shaped and graced by God in worship. This alone allows our worship to move from perfunctory and boring (in any musical style) to awesome and inviting; complacency is bad for evangelism as well as bad for our own souls. But to let our liturgy and music open depths and heights of human hearts to God, to let it open *our* hearts and let this love pour forth in our breath and voices and song and lives and world—this is amazing grace indeed.

Prayer practices
Tracing our desire
Praise overflows from hearts fully open to the One who is our heart's deepest desire. The praise that music expresses and evokes, reaching

through and beyond words and melody to open our entire being to God, spills forth spontaneously—indeed rapturously—the more fully we are in touch with this deepest desire of our hearts. Often we fear our desires, afraid they will lead to destruction or gluttony, infantile rages enacted. Yet ultimately, as beings created in the image of God, we trust that the deepest desires of our hearts do not lead us away from God but toward and into God. Of course, layers of false and distorted desire obscure these authentic core desires of the heart. Thus the spiritual practice of tracing desire becomes all the more important as it helps us distinguish life-giving from false desires, those which connect us more deeply to God and those which lead us away from the One whose praise is our highest joy.

In the practice of examen we began to learn daily attentiveness to the fine-grained texture of our experience. As we engage this prayer form, day after day, week after month after year, we notice patterns to this experience. That is, we might notice that gratitude often emerges in particular places in our day: with a certain person, in a particular kind of encounter, during times of rest, time outdoors, or in prayer. Paying attention to these places of gratitude, and to the other places we sense God present (or absent) in our day's experience, begins to evoke new desire as well. "I want more of this happy connection, or I want to avoid this person, this unpleasant experience. I want so-and-so to notice me. I want to be the star! I want to experience love like I did today every day. I want more play time. I want to make a difference to people in need."

The practice of praying with our desires is an invitation not simply to notice these desires emerging, but actually to pray them. Tell your real desires honestly to God. Of course not all desires are mature nor particularly Christian; you may feel embarrassed or even ashamed at some of them. That's okay—pray them anyway, and see what happens. And remember: refrain from self-attack! There's no need to tell God in advance how ridiculous your desires are; just pray them. You may be surprised how God receives them (and you). For, like it or not, our desires are in many ways *who we are;* they are signposts of where our hearts are presently living in all immediacy. Do not expect them to be fully mature in Christ. Nor are our desires cast in stone, but like the rest of us they need forming and shaping through long-term immersion in *God's* desires and love and leading. See which desires deepen in prayer and draw you closer to God, perhaps quite unexpectedly, and which lead you away from God into envy or obsession—ultimately into despair. Bringing our desires into prayer both deepens intimacy with God, sharing with God who we really are and what we really long for, and allows God to cleanse and shape our hearts themselves by drawing our honest desires close to God, opening them more and more to God's desires for our joy, peace, and freedom and that of the whole world. Only by bringing our inmost heart to God can we experience both love and liberation at that deepest core level of ourselves where desire lives. Ultimately your desire, deepened, stripped raw, and transformed, will draw close to God in nearly unbearable joy: your vocation. In chapter 8 we will return to questions of vocation and discernment as a culminating practice of the Christian life. This practice of praying our desires is an essential building block for discernment.

The arts as play and prayer

As we become conscious of ever deeper desires of our hearts we find ourselves drawn into that praise John Newton experienced that comes when we indeed "follow our bliss" into the heart of God in Jesus Christ. When we are most closely in touch with our profound need of God, our heart's passionate longing for God, our whole being desiring to see and hear and know and touch and fall in love with God, and live out God's mercy and justice and joy in the real world, our song can truly soar, our praise open from the very roots of our being. Newton wrote many hymns in addition to "Amazing grace." He found the praise flowing from his heart's desire expanding into music and poetry. So too, for countless generations, have artists and children who are in touch with the beauty and awe and pain and mystery of created life. When we sing in church we participate in this astonishing outpouring of praise; for some of us it is the only active participation in the arts we experience in any given week.

How impoverished we are! For all the arts are potential windows into new experience of God through our senses, emotions, bodies, and souls. Children often spend hours immersed in projects of various kinds: drawing or finger-painting, making mud pies or other sculptures out of natural objects or play dough, singing or drumming or dancing. As adults, many of us think we have lost this ability to engage in art or play but, in fact, a re-connection with the practice of art can help to open creative or playful or expressive parts of ourselves that are not lost at all but simply submerged. Jesus says, "unless you change and become like children, you will never enter the kingdom of heaven" (Matt. 18:3). Theologians debate what he meant by this; but certainly for those who have lost touch with childhood pleasure in art, color, texture, sound, movement—in sheer creative expressiveness done for the fun of it and without judgment or criticism—immersion in the arts can indeed help open long-lost dimensions of ourselves to God. As children and other artists and musicians know, time spent immersed in creative activity is not "wasted" time at all. It draws you into a different reality, where you may be surprised at the feelings that emerge. If you have small children, or grandchildren, or other young relatives or friends nearby, you can perhaps find ways to play with art simply by learning from them, playing with them. But even if you don't often spend time with children, you can still relearn the joy of the arts, either as play or in more disciplined forms of practice.

I will focus here more on play than on full-fledged artistic practice because of the value of play itself in our lives and prayer. But, of course, for those skilled in particular art forms, disciplined practice itself begins to verge into play as one lets go into the beauty or movement or color at hand. As in spiritual disciplines, the discipline of learning an artistic practice can become transparent over time to the living presence of God. To learn an art form new to you, take a class. Drawing or painting, quilting or weaving or pottery: which of these sparks joy in you or takes you back to your favorite childhood play? Join a choir. Take up woodworking, especially forms that evoke creativity as well as craft. Start a writing circle. Attend poetry readings and see if the images you hear spark your imagination. Or something else entirely: kite-making! Flower arranging! Whatever! Regardless of what you choose, let it be something truly fun and pleasurable for you; something you can do without non-stop judgment or evaluation; and something that evokes expressiveness of some kind, to foster deeper connection with your feelings and with God.

In the process, try engaging with your artistic play as a form of prayer, rooted in and in turn opening up into prayer. The main thing is to begin your art/play with prayer, open to God whatever feelings or experiences you notice along the way, and then explore with God whatever emerges in the artwork itself, entrusting to the Holy Spirit all the gifts, however "useless" they may seem, of the time spent. Here is an example, using drawing. (You can substitute whatever activity you are attracted to. It doesn't have to be a "spiritual"-sounding project.)

Drawing play: Begin with prayer, returning in your memory to a place you experienced God's presence. Rest in God as long as you wish. When you're ready, take a large piece of paper and draw circles to represent dimensions of your spirituality: your relationships with friends and loved ones, with yourself/your body, the earth, the church, the world/society, and God. You may have other circles as well. Make various circles large or small, in proportion to their significance for you; perhaps they overlap or are connected in different ways, or perhaps some sit off by themselves. Perhaps some are different colors or contain symbols, etc. You can create an image *either* of what you sense is your real present spirituality *or* what you long for. In either case, let this be a playful process and itself a form of openness to God's surprising gifts. Don't worry about how round your circles are or how realistic the symbols you draw are. Instead, try to let go—use big swooping gestures if you want, bright or splashy or thick dark colors, intensity of scribble or grace and fluidity of line. Pray as you go along and try to sense how the particular images or connections or symbols feel to you even as you are drawing them, what resonance they carry for you. What is God like in the picture? Bring all these feelings to God, and stay with God as long as you like. Sign and date your work.

For reflection, discussion, journaling, or spiritual direction

1. What is your favorite hymn? What do you love about it? What memories does it spark?
2. What is your favorite sung portion of the liturgy? What do you love about it? What musical setting of the liturgy do you most enjoy using to sing this portion?
3. What is your earliest memory of music of any kind? Of music in church? If you joined the church as an older child, teenager, or adult, what were your early impressions of church music? Have those shifted over time, and if so in what ways?
4. How does your congregation help children learn the church's song and prayers? How does your congregation help visitors similarly learn their way into your sung prayer?
5. What music or other sounds do you listen to from day to day? If someone who did not know you heard this "soundtrack" of your life, would it give an accurate glimpse of your faith and identity?
6. Does the practice of praying with your desires attract you, scare you, repel you? Are there desires of your heart you truly long to explore further?
7. What is your favorite form of art? Do you regularly immerse yourself in art? Do you *practice* any forms of art? If so, how does this practice shape your prayer? How might you like to play more in your life?
8. Where in this chapter did you sense the Spirit moving in you? Return to that word, sentence, or paragraph and listen for where your heart is being stirred. Bring your feelings, questions, or responses to God in prayer and/or journaling.

5
Silence before the Word

Silence is invited at various places throughout the service: before the prelude, following the invitation to confession, following each reading and the sermon, during the prayers of intercession and communion, before the benediction. Sometimes, as between "Let us pray" and the prayer that follows, this silence may be simply an extended pause, a holy moment to catch our breath and help each person collectively arrive in the presence of God. At other times, such as following the sermon, we may receive the gift of a minute or more of silence to let the Word reach deep into our hearts and take root there. If we are lucky and in a congregation attuned to the necessity of silence for deepening into God, we will be allowed to experience several or even all of those named above, Sunday after Sunday. In some parishes, however, nervous presiders or musicians rush through these pauses and silences, afraid people will get anxious or bored if nothing seems to be going on.

It is true that the good and fruitful use of silence is an acquired capacity; for most people it does not come naturally. Most of us must learn over time what to do with extended or even short silences in worship, how to let them become openings to deeper prayer rather than dead time. Many parishes find it helpful to make this learning an intentional process for people. This might include regular reference to silence and its fruits in preaching, or classes to teach prayer forms conducive to deepening the use of silence (such as some of those forms detailed in this book), or simply by inviting people into this ongoing liturgical practice of rest together in the word, letting newcomers and children learn from those more experienced with the grace of silence inviting us all into God. However it is done, we truly need these spaces where "nothing" is going on.

We live in a world relentless in its drivenness, its insistence on always pushing ahead to the next new thing, the next stimulation, the next entertainment or achievement. We become dulled to our own interior lives, accustomed to numbing them away with distractions, busyness, media stimulation, or addictions. Feeling pressured to achieve and perform, we resist spending time—even five minutes a day!—in silence with God. It feels like a waste of time, and those unaccustomed to the interior rhythms of worship often expect even liturgy to follow the same rigid hour-long time blocks into which the *TV Guide* has patterned our lives. If we sit in silence for a full minute after the sermon, we might be late getting to brunch! We'll miss the kick-off of the game! So utterly do we program our existence that even a few seconds—let alone an entire minute—of silence with God feels like a violation of our busy schedules.

But the resistance goes deeper. There's a reason we have scheduled ourselves into oblivion, a reason we fill our down time with TV on the couch or talk radio in the car or computer chat rooms at night, alongside regular pursuit of chocolate or alcohol, stimulation or retail consumption or self-improvement. We may complain endlessly about being overworked, and may mean it quite sincerely, yet refuse to create for ourselves even small openings into rest and silence in our busy lives. We may even fill our exercise or dog-walking hours with CDs and headphones to keep from getting "bored" by time spent simply outdoors. This compulsive busyness is a problem not only for adults. Books have been written on the loss of empty spaces even in childhood—those hours of nothing to do previous generations of children experienced in the interstices of the busiest farm or city family life, where exploration of the surroundings or simple endless day-dreaming gave them regular access to their interior and exterior worlds.

I believe there is a reason for this wholesale withdrawal from the experience of silence in our society—much as we may lament its loss—and that it has to do with resistance to deeper levels of our beings: unwanted feelings, intuitions, desires, or needs. As we saw in the chapter on confession, we are cut off from others, from ourselves, from God, from the earth, and this hurts so profoundly we can't bear to face it. To the extent we are resisting the One who shows up in our depths, we often run from silence as well. The literature on prayer and spiritual growth throughout Christian history is full of examples about the difficulty of sustaining authentic silence—silence encompassing actual emptiness, including space for God—in the midst of nonstop internal chatter and distractions. Of all the practices outlined in this book, it's possible that silence in its various forms is the most difficult for late-modern Western individuals. For this reason I have located it at the center of the book, at its heart. Silence is not the most central practice of prayer and worship; the chapters on word and sacraments describe the ways we most reliably and transparently receive the living presence and love of God in Jesus Christ. But silence—authentic, terrifying emptiness—is a necessary condition for being able to receive these gifts in the first place.

This is not a matter of works-righteousness. I in no way intend to say that the practice of silence is some divine prerequisite establishing our worthiness of grace, nor that those incapable of silence are somehow barred from knowing God or being saved. But just as we find it hard to connect with people who only talk and refuse ever to listen, or who are so busy and active that they never have time to spend with us, so it is with God. Our journey of growth in love includes learning to be ever more fully available to God too—and this simple *availability to God*, rather than any "works," is the heart of authentic silence. To receive God's word depends on our ceasing to talk (or plug our ears, or otherwise run away) long enough, and deeply enough, to be able to truly *listen* to God. And while strict requirements of fasting before communion are less widely observed than in the past, still receiving the eucharist at the depths God desires to nourish us depends too on being in touch with our deepest hungers, the emptiness at the heart of ourselves—that emptiness we are running from when we fill ourselves with chocolate or overwork. Silence and actually experiencing our own emptiness, our own poverty, can be frightening indeed; at its heart our silence is a way of dropping our defenses and making ourselves utterly available to God.

Thus the practices of silence are essentially quite simple. They are forms by which we grow in availability of the heart. Many classics of Christian spirituality circle around this mystery of learning silence before God. Some writers speak of a way of *nothingness*, of God's utter ineffability and transcendence of every human category, so that we approach God not solely through words or images, but through the negation of every name, every image of the divine mystery. This tradition seeks to empty the mind and heart of categories which limit the mystery of God. Texts like *The Cloud of Unknowing* manifest this approach. Similarly, texts which deal with "dark night" experiences point to the awesome revelation of God in human experience most powerfully *not* in our mountaintop moments but precisely in those experiences of God's apparent absence and our own doubt or feelings of abandonment. St. John of the Cross's *Dark Night of the Soul* is a classic example of this motif, inviting us when these experiences loom in our lives not to flee from them or suppress them but to embrace them as best we can, to let the dark night itself strip us of old, inadequate conceptions of God and patterns of life. Gradually, mysteriously, often in ways or forms we least expect, we may be opened to new and very different experiences of reality.

Christian texts exploring these motifs center around a third cluster of themes: poverty, emptiness, and humility. We don't necessarily like these themes. Who wants to live in *poverty*? Certainly not those who are themselves poor; and are we not commanded to help them escape their poverty? Similarly, *emptiness* is a condition so unpleasant we avoid it at all costs. Biologically hardwired to fill ourselves whenever food is available, we simply do so, and we let this aversion to emptiness carry over into the internal emotional/psychic arena as well. And *humility* smacks of humiliation. For those already confused about their worth, such as those who have survived trauma, abuse, or violence, the mere mention of humility can evoke a tyrannical God intent on crushing our wills, our individuality, our power.

All these latter themes from Christian tradition have fallen on difficult times in our contemporary milieu. Confrontation with our mortality, our emptiness, our unmet needs threatens to dissolve the false constructs of self and nation and world we think constitute us. And as fragile human beings perhaps we *can't* finally enter the awesome humility of availability before God on our own. In fact, far from being some kind of "work," perhaps even the capacity for silence is already the fruit of grace stirring in us. Without it we turn away; we rustle our bulletins during tiny pauses in the service, whisper to our neighbors throughout communion. On our own we can't ever fully stop, relax, drop our bulletins, open our hands, and sink into silence. But Jesus can. And he invites us to follow—or, better, to meet him where he already is.

For Jesus is born not only into the ordinariness and excitement of our humanity. He is born into our darkness, into that dark night, that poverty, that emptiness we flee at all costs. Born in the dark, in the cold, in a shack unfit for human habitation, he lives with no place to call home, embraces sinners and outcasts, ends up in a criminal's death and a stranger's tomb, even descending into hell. In him every poverty of our experience is encompassed. In him the darkness is embraced. He is the One in and through whom alone we have the courage to put down our crutch and descend into our own darkness, our emptiness and radical hunger, our mortality, and our own radical availability to God once all the masks and distractions and social roles are stripped away. Baptized and welcomed, confessing and forgiven, our hearts opened to praise and love beyond our imaginings, we have the courage in Jesus Christ to enter at last the silence at our center. And there, in utter poverty, we learn that sweetest of all gifts: to cherish the Beloved alone, to depend for our very lives on his leading, to cling to him forever.

Prayer practices
Centering prayer
Centering prayer is a practice making use of a sacred word as a focus for prayer. It has to do with receptivity to God, willingness, adoration, letting go, radical openness to God. As we move into silence, we are often plagued by distracting thoughts, the urgent noise of our ordinary lives churning away at high volume. We may quickly feel inadequate in praying, unable to focus on God in the face of this relentless internal noise, and think we should give up. Yet in centering prayer even distractions become an invitation to keep returning to God. They are not "problems" as much as more of ourselves to offer to God. To welcome *and* keep releasing all thoughts back into the sacred word both signals and enacts our desire to let God embrace every dimension of our being in each moment.

Four steps of centering prayer, plus one more for Sunday:
1. Choose a sacred word as a symbol of your intention to open to and welcome God's presence and action in your life (or a tactile metaphor like being held in God's arms). Words can include Jesus' name, "Abba" (or "Imma"), or a dimension of God such as "peace," "mercy," "light": anything that reminds your heart of God's presence and love. In Russian Orthodox

spirituality, praying the Jesus Prayer ("Lord Jesus Christ, Son of God, have mercy on me") is a central practice. People use shorter sections of the prayer as well, perhaps the most common being simply "Jesus." To pray with Jesus' name is powerful and intimate, but you may prefer another name for God as well. For instance, Thomas Merton, a well-known twentieth-century monk, gives us the following image of God: "Mercy within mercy within mercy." Use the name that best invites *you* close to the Beloved of your heart.

2. Find a place to sit comfortably where you won't be disturbed for twenty minutes. Close your eyes, let yourself relax, and gradually quiet your breathing as you begin to rest in God. Silently welcome your sacred word as your receiving of God's presence; let it repeat itself slowly in you, over and over, without any particular effort.

3. When thoughts or feelings, memories or fantasies emerge (which they will), don't berate yourself or try to force them out of your awareness. Receive them gently and let them go into God, returning over and over to the name of God you are using in prayer. If concerns for people in need emerge, release them to God. If you remember some urgent task, jot a note and return to prayer. Patterns of thoughts may signal some deeper need God is inviting you to open. Overall, when you notice new thoughts emerging, don't follow them or let them entangle you right now; simply bring them to God and release them. Gentleness is key. God is endlessly, exquisitely gentle with you.

4. With your sacred word, let yourself learn over time to rest completely in God. This is your chance each day to grow more and more open to the light, life, and love God longs to pour into your heart. It's pure receptivity, pure mercy and grace. Soak it in. And at the end of twenty to thirty minutes, gradually let yourself return to ordinary life.

5. *Sunday step:* On Sunday, try to arrive early for worship and begin centering prayer before the service begins. Do so (as always!) not in a rigid way, chastising yourself or others if this is more difficult than at home, but simply as a way to let worship itself become a place where you enter the deepening internal silence with God that centering prayer invites. As the service goes on, try to stay in prayer, returning to your sacred word if you notice your mind wandering from worship. Here the purpose of this word is to keep returning you to the service itself. Try to notice what in each Sunday's readings, hymns, prayers, or ritual movement opens you more deeply to God's living presence and also where you get distracted. Bring these experiences to prayer.

Variant: Walking meditation. Walking meditation can mean simply walking, paying attention to colors, smells, birds, trees, weather, human presence, light and shadow, and letting yourself go in sheer presence to God in it all. Do this as often as possible, whenever you have five or ten minutes or an entire day inviting you outdoors. Walk to errands. Linger along the way. Creation itself is a primordial gift of God, and our hearts and bodies need time in it. Be as entirely present as you can to this breath, this step, that flower or person. You can let your walking draw you more fully into your breath: breathe slowly and deeply, perhaps taking in some aspect of God with each breath (peace, presence, beauty, love) and releasing some aspect of your life's burdens, fears, or tightness with each exhale. Or try centering prayer as a walking rather than a sitting practice. In this case, as above, simply let a sacred word be the symbol of your heart's desire to rest in God, to be utterly open to God. Keep returning to this word as you walk, letting all you see and experience on your walk draw you deeper into the mercy of God.

Fasting

Like silence for those unaccustomed to it, fasting can be a frightening prospect. We may know intellectually that an occasional respite from the nonstop consumption of our lives could be helpful—perhaps, we think, in some masochistic, bracing way—but we resist actually carrying it out. Even for well-fed Americans the terror of famine, of poverty, is not far beneath the surface. In addition, ubiquitous media portrayals of idealized bodies—especially female bodies—have brought concerns with body image and thinness into high relief. For some, the prospect of fasting may reinforce an internalized sense of themselves as not worthy of being fed: now a punitive "God" is siding with the media commanding them to be thinner. And for those who grew up in true poverty with real shortages of food, fasting may still be too painful.

Yet for all of us, in any of these situations, fasting of some sort is an essential discipline of the Christian life. For many of us who are healthy and well-fed, short fasts from food provide an embodied way to enact and experience deeper levels of our emptiness before God, while simultaneously easing the strain of overconsumption on our bodies and releasing resources for the hungry (check with your doctor if you have concerns about fasting). For others, such as those with a history of food-related deprivation, or those for whom food and its presence or absence hold no particular existential weight, there may be other forms of fasting that would be more helpful spiritually. For instance, recovering addicts find the daily practice of abstinence from the substance they crave drawing them into intense reliance on a Higher Power. Their abstinence includes also refraining from many kinds of self-punitive thoughts or behaviors or obsessive forms of control. For someone else, fasting from TV or computer games might similarly open up raw, empty time before God as compulsively driven forms of behavior are gradually withdrawn. For you, it may be something else entirely, something on which you have become dependent which alienates you from God, yourself, or others, and from which you sense God inviting you to fast. Once again, the practice of examen (chapter 3) can be of immense help. Over time with this prayer form you may notice some aspect of your life, relationships, behavior, or mental furniture that consistently alienates you from God. Day after day, or whenever it recurs, this habit or relational pattern or substance shows up in that part of the day where you found yourself far from God, resisting God, or feeling desolate, lonely, or conflicted. This can be a very important clue to something you might be well-served fasting from. Depending on the substance or problem, this could be a short-term fast, perhaps during Lent, or an attempt to turn from this behavior entirely. Regardless, the language of fasting can help.

In all cases, whether you are fasting from food or from some other substance or behavior, fasting should always be accompanied by prayer. The empty stomach, the frightening void that begins to open when a genuine fast is begun, is intended for God. And this is the case *not* in order to impress God or to compound our holiness (fasting + prayer = a truly exemplary Christian!), but because of our enormous need at precisely these places of emptying. This is a place where we feel particularly fragile and needy of support (or why else this compulsive behavior in the first place?) that we are now trying to open to God's healing care. Thus, in order that fasting not become some sort of works-righteousness or otherwise self-punishing, it needs to be conducted always, only, within the mercy and tenderness and embrace of God. For instance, if you are fasting one day or meal a week during Lent, let those meal times be spent with God so that you can bring all the feelings and needs that emerge directly into prayer, and so that you can be well and deeply loved in your hunger. Let your need open you to others who hunger too, that it may deepen your compassion and response to them. But let this not be punitive toward yourself. Be more gentle with yourself than usual in these times, and try to sense God's exquisite gentleness with you.

Fasting is very hard. But the emerging openness to the desires lodged far beneath the surface of your usual existence, and to reality in many forms, makes these periods of withdrawal priceless. Certainly fasting from your compulsions will give you more time with God, yourself, the earth, and others—think of the time you spend! But a real fast from some idol of your heart also opens you to God on a level of need you simply couldn't otherwise touch. It helps God cleanse you and claim you in ways otherwise impossible. That is, it opens you to an interior silence receptive to the loving and living Word.

For reflection, discussion, journaling, or spiritual direction

1. Do you seek out silence, or flee it at all costs? In your experience, does God "live" in silence?

2. Would you appreciate more silence in worship? Less? At what points in particular?

3. Where would you most like or need more silence in your life outside worship?

4. If you generally flee silence in your life, why do you think that is?

5. Have you ever experienced a "dark night" time in your life? Do you have a sense now of where God was in that experience?

6. If you already practice—or are now trying—centering prayer, what do you find most life-giving about it? Where do you struggle most?

7. Is there some substance, behavior, relationship, or pattern in your life from which God may be inviting you to fast? What feelings emerge as you consider this possibility?

8. Where in this chapter did you sense the Spirit moving in you? Return to that word, sentence, or paragraph and listen for where your heart is being stirred. Bring your feelings, questions, or responses to God in prayer and/or journaling.

6
Receiving the Living Word

The first half of the eucharistic liturgy centers on word: scripture and proclamation. The church quite rightly speaks of word and sacrament as twin centers of the liturgy. Each draws us close to Jesus Christ, God's living Word, our bread from heaven. Word and sacrament are not separate or separable. Holy communion is not an optional addendum tacked on now and then to a service of scripture and proclamation. Neither are readings and proclamation mere warm-ups, like pre-game verbiage before the real event gets underway. Rather than two separate ritual events, word and sacrament are one: our receiving in mind and heart and flesh and blood the living Lord who loves us and desires to draw close in precisely the ways we each and all most need. We feast on this Word *pro me,* for you, for all here and now—his very being poured out—in readings and proclamation preached and sung. We feast on that very same Word in the bread and wine of his flesh.

Our capacity to *hear this Word* is thus vital to our experience of worship. For Martin Luther, hearing this Word means a personal encounter with the God who endlessly "speaks" Christ as Word. The biblical text proclaimed in readings and sermon becomes revelatory, becomes Word of God in all reality, when (and only when) through it Jesus Christ is made alive in the hearts of hearers. We don't simply hear the scriptures as stories or doctrines, however entertaining or informative; we hear them as personal address. That is, we hear the words of scripture proclaimed that they may become transparent to the real presence of Jesus himself, right here, addressing us in person, individually and together. It is the Holy Spirit working through spoken human words who makes the living Word himself alive in and among us: God speaking *to me, to us*. When we truly hear this living Word it catches fire. God's Word—Jesus—has power right in the "speaking," right in the experience of encounter with him. This Word of God is living and active (Heb. 4:12), actually enacting in real life what it promises. Watch out! This Word will transform you, if you let it come close.

This is true of all the scriptures read in worship: Old Testament (Hebrew scriptures), psalm, epistle, and gospel. As God's word, each has the power to become transparent to the living Word, Jesus Christ, addressing you. Thus we are invited to hear scripture not as a static text of fixed meanings, the same for all ages and all people, nor in terms of how other people we know ought to be hearing it, but written *for us* like a letter—in fact, a love letter. In scripture God's love is poured out for us, and we linger over these lines as lovers do over the precious words their beloved writes them.

Of course this is not meant simplistically. The living Word is not synonymous with the words on a page. There is no denying that some biblical texts have been used to hurt people. In some cases, we may in fact resist the verbal message of the text, but as we do so *within* contemplative reading then even the words resisted—or rather, the One who alone animates words into Word—can draw us close to God precisely in our struggle with individual passages. Luther reminds us that it isn't the book itself, the words on the page, that is the Word of God, but Jesus Christ; and biblical passages that do not convey

Christ are not automatically revelatory. In prayer, then, you do not somehow have to hear every word as meant for you; rather, you are learning to listen for the *living Word*, Jesus Christ himself alive and addressing you through these words—occasionally even in ways that seem to move against the grain of the passage itself.

We experience this process of drawing close to Jesus Christ as Word throughout the Bible. In fact, we need the thick complexity of the entire scripture, from Genesis to Revelation and all those strange or mysterious or wonderful texts in between, in order to hear Christ the Word in all fullness. In particular, however, the gospel stories draw us close to Jesus himself. They record the words, actions, and presence of Jesus to his disciples, the crowds, sick people and lepers, enemies and authorities. Thus these stories have a particular resonance for prayer and provide many windows for our contemplative entrance into the story, into actual encounter with Jesus himself. For example, in hearing of Simon Peter's first encounter with Jesus in Luke 5 at the beginning of this book, we may experience this story as our invitation into Jesus' showing up in *our* lives. Through these stories we enter the *ongoing* mystery of God's self-revelation in Jesus Christ to each of us and all of our world. Like Luke 5, gospel stories can become occasions for *your* present encounter with Jesus and the opportunity for heart-to-heart presence with him. As you learn to experience and express to him the feelings, needs, desires, or reactions the gospel stories evoke in you, and to listen in turn for his responses to you, intimacy of a most healing sort slowly takes root. In time, this relationship will draw you ever more fully into him—and your own true self.

Thus the goal of truly hearing the Word is deepening encounter and intimacy with Jesus and the triune God he embodies. Centered in gospel stories, this encounter expands to take place through any of the scripture texts read on Sunday, for Jesus Christ *is* the Word of God "speaking" through all of scripture and, very often, through several of the texts for the day as they are proclaimed alongside one another. One of the great joys of worshiping following the appointed pattern of readings in the lectionary is hearing God opening up not only in particular individual readings but precisely in the juxtaposition of texts: Old Testament and epistle, psalm and gospel, interpreting or deepening or subverting one another in ways entirely impossible to predict within the hearing of each worshiper. Learning to hear the Word means learning to pray in ways that open your heart to Jesus' living presence in, with, and under these living words, in whatever ways he desires to draw close to you. It's about learning to "listen to him," the Beloved, over and over and over in our lives, as the voice of God so graciously invites us at Jesus' transfiguration (compare Mark 9:7 and parallels).

This is *prayer as relationship*, prayer as mutual self-disclosure, whose sole purpose is love. And it is an engagement in relationship that is far from passive. Rather than merely hearing scripture, we are invited to pay attention to the places it echoes in us, the places we resist, the feelings stirred up, the desires and fears and hopes and memories a particular word or story evokes—and to bring those deepest reactions back into prayer. This is how we grow in trust with Jesus—by bringing him the actual responses of our whole being to the scripture we hear, pouring this all out to him, and then paying attention to his own response in turn. Scripture and proclamation become then an opening for this real-time engagement with Jesus in and through the events of biblical stories as these echo in our very particular hearts. And, just as in ordinary human relationships of love, this is precisely how intimacy is developed, each person opening to the other more and more of his or her actual feelings, reactions, needs, desires, and love. You will get to know Jesus as a real person, as One who is truly speaking to you, listening to you, engaged with you, and transforming you in the most tender and powerful love you need.

Prayer practices

Both prayer practices described in this chapter can be done either as individual or as group exercises. An advantage of group experience is that the presence of more experienced pray-ers can help beginners stay present to the Word for longer periods than they might manage on their own. Group leaders should not only be experienced in group leadership but sufficiently grounded in these prayer forms that they can lead intuitively, with a sensitivity to the Spirit's movements in the present moment so as to help the group move to deeper levels of engagement with the living Word in its midst.

Lectio divina

Lectio divina ("divine reading") is an ancient monastic prayer form that has influenced nearly every major Western Christian tradition in spirituality, including Martin Luther (for more on Luther's prayer, including a contemporary re-working of *lectio divina*, see http://www.dailytext.com/dailytexts/TRIP.php). This practice encompasses four stages inviting prayerful reading of scripture. It can be used with short appointed lessons for each day, such as the *Daily Texts* of the Moravian tradition; with a single book of the Bible over time; or throughout the week using the lessons for the upcoming Sunday. However the biblical passages are chosen for one's reading, the process is the same. Its most important elements are the heart's quiet listening for where God is moving as Word and the freedom to linger there with God in whatever ways the Spirit may direct. This is reading scripture for formation, not for *in*formation: not to cover as many chapters as possible in a week, or to derive new insights into, say, Pauline doctrine, but simply to listen for the Word of God for you, today.

a. *Lectio*. This stage simply means "reading." In ancient times people did not read silently; *reading* meant reading aloud. Just as in worship we notice new elements in the text when we hear it read aloud in a particular human voice and inflection, so too in *lectio* it can be fruitful to read your text out loud and not only silently. This allows you to listen to the words with both your inner and your outer ears. Thus this first stage is already intended to draw you into the presence of the living Word. Practices of silence such as centering prayer, even for a few minutes, can be a helpful way to prepare for your reading in *lectio*. After reading the text silently or aloud, let it echo in you a while—very gently, without any pressure to come up with anything in particular—before reading it again. The second time through (or if you have strong reactions already the first time), pay attention to places the text particularly calls to you or tugs at your heart. Are there words or phrases that leap off the page or where your heart responds in some way? Sometimes this may be a movement of joy or gratitude, and at other times a place where something in the text bothers you. When you notice this, stop. Now it is time to let the text draw you deeper into itself.

b. *Meditatio*. The word "meditation" is close to the *ruminating* that cows do, placidly chewing their cud. Once the Word has begun to move in you, stay there. The point is not to get through the passage, but to follow wherever the Spirit leads. Stay with the word or phrase that tugs at you, repeating it and returning to it when distractions pull you away. If this word eventually dries up, return to the passage and continue reading until, again, your heart is caught by a word or phrase in which you are invited to abide a while. Again, there is no force or strain suggested in this process, no urgency to come up with some moral or lesson from the enterprise. You are simply spending time in the Word. As you abide there, let your mind wander within it. What stirs in your intuition, your memories? What experiences from your past, hopes for your future, or feelings from your present does this text, this word, this image evoke? Listen for these just as you listen for the stirrings of the Spirit in the text, and let them be part of one reality: your life, your feelings and hopes and experience, all held within this Word. Savor this time and listen for the heart of Christ revealed in it, in you.

c. *Oratio (prayer)*. Here we begin to move into actual response to these movements of God. This is noted as a third stage, but of course in reality you may be beginning to give voice to feelings or questions or reactions to what the Word is stirring in you all along the way. This is fine as long as you are providing plenty of space for deepening meditation with the Word and extended interior listening to what stirs in you, not rushing straight into your own speech. Be sure that you are indeed allowing this depth of meditation, for the prayer at this third stage means responding to God from the *heart*, not the head. And for most of us, to let the Word descend all the way into our heart takes time. Here, then, is where your heart touched or moved or opened or questioning expresses itself to the Lord, particularly on the feeling level. Note that this means on the level of your *real* feelings, not what you think a pious Christian "ought" to be feeling in response to a given text. This point is crucial and can hardly be overstated. The degree of honesty with which you bring God your *real* feelings determines the depth of intimacy you will be able to experience.

For instance, in the story of the prodigal son (Luke 15:11-32) you might feel obliged to give thanks to God for being so generous and welcoming of sinners, like the father in the story. Surely that is the correct response to the text, the one Jesus is encouraging. However, suppose in reality that as you were reading this story today you felt a jolt of annoyance at your coworker. She has been blowing off her job, leaving you to pick up the pieces and get all the work done, and what's more, the boss doesn't seem to notice but treats her as the favorite—just like the father with his wayward son! If you merely stick to the "right" response to this text, it is likely to leave you feeling flat and bored in prayer: "Thank you God for being so kind and gracious to all us sinners. Got that done; time for lunch." However, perhaps you notice your annoyance in the story and are able to tell Jesus about your coworker, even though you are afraid this puts you in the position of the older brother in the story, the one who is typically portrayed as having the wrong attitude. In this case, bringing Jesus *both* your problem at work and your fear of his condemnation for being unforgiving, you will probably find powerful things happening in prayer with this text. Whatever happens, you are unlikely to be bored or to find prayer flat and God distant—precisely because you have the courage to let the Word open you to God in all trust and honesty *right in the places it is stirring in you.*

d. *Contemplatio.* In the previous example of praying with the story of the prodigal son, in light of your work situation much could transpire in that prayer. You might experience Jesus leaving the party and coming out to the field to listen to you as you pour out your experience and feelings of resentment at your workplace. You might sense him taking you by the hand, or giving you some new perspective on your coworker, or suggesting a way to conduct yourself differently at work. You might perceive him leading you away from this place altogether and into a community that is better suited to your vocation. Or, having vented your long-suppressed "sinful" feelings to this One who turns out to be love itself, *for you,* right in this mess, you might be astonished to find that the intimacy of his gaze and attention to you, right here where your life hurts, is so healing that your coworker slowly recedes in importance in your interior world and Jesus himself comes closer and closer, loving you with such mercy and passion that you find yourself caught up entirely in his love. This is *contemplatio:* the moments where prayer reaching to our depths dissolves utterly into presence, and we are quite amazingly brought close to the very heart of God. This experience can be rare or more frequent, fleeting or sustained; it is the manna our hearts long for, the chance to rest at the very core of one's being in the actual living presence of God, to gaze on the face of Jesus beholding us with such unbelievable love. To live in him, listen to him, discover and follow where he is leading, and worship him whose love is our life: this is the Christian way. It is our heart's desire.

Ignatian contemplative prayer

Begin as in *lectio,* above. This is a variant of *lectio divina* focused on gospel texts in particular (for instance, you might choose to pray with the gospel for the upcoming Sunday). In Ignatian prayer we become actors in a particular gospel story, invited to become the ones healed and called, taught and transformed, those resisting and questioning, drawing close or keeping our distance. This requires setting the stage. As you are reading the story, use your imagination as fully as possible to evoke the scene described. This is an important component of the process. It's very sensory: visualize the landscape, the village, the street or lake or room or hill where the story you're reading takes place. What color are the wildflowers along the road? What's the weather like? Are there birds nearby? What do the people look like? Notice the smells, sounds, noises, textures, and emotional climate of the story. Do you smell smoke from a cook-fire, or the perfume filling the house when Jesus is anointed? The more sensory detail you can imagine, the more vividly you will be able to enter the story. Don't worry that you're "making it all up"; of course you are. If you approach the process with the desire to meet Jesus, the Spirit will guide you through your unconscious, and what you make up in the process may prove pivotal to your prayer itself.

Next, move more deeply into the story and consider where in the scene you sense yourself located today. Are you one of the main characters? A disciple? A bystander? A Pharisee? Depending on what's going on in your life and where the Holy Spirit wants to move in your prayer, you may turn out to be anyone: gender doesn't necessarily matter, nor age or any other logical consideration. You might be someone not even mentioned in the story: a woman in a story full of men, or yourself in real life at the foot of the cross. Or you may even be non-human: the boat Jesus enters, a donkey at the manger. Don't place yourself *as* Jesus but as someone with him in the story. Then, from the vantage point of whoever and wherever you are in the story, pay attention to all that's going on around you. Who is doing what? What are people saying to Jesus? How does he respond? What do you notice in his face, voice, eyes, touch, body language as he reacts to people and the situation?

Finally, as in *oratio* above, begin to engage with Jesus directly in prayer. This is the heart of Ignatian contemplative prayer, what St. Ignatius called the *colloquy:* to talk to Jesus as you would to your closest friend. Once again, this is *not* telling Jesus what you think you're supposed to feel about the story but what you *really* feel. Tell him all this. See how he responds. How does he listen to you? Does he ask or say anything? What is his voice like, his face? What further feelings or desire does his reaction elicit in you? Can you express these to him? What happens next? Take as much time as you want, and keep bringing your *real* experience in each moment to Jesus, letting him love you and responding to his love.

For reflection, discussion, journaling, or spiritual direction

1. What are your favorite Bible passages or stories? Why?
2. Dietrich Bonhoeffer described scripture as a love letter from God. Do you hear scripture as addressed to you by God? How does this image help you hear the Word differently?
3. To which of the prayer practices outlined here do you feel more drawn? How do you imagine these practices helping you engage with God around "difficult" passages of scripture?
4. Have you ever had an experience of encounter with Jesus through your reading or hearing of scripture? What happened? Did the experience surprise you, change you, disturb you, console you?
5. How might contemplative listening to the Word deepen your experience of worship? Are there ways your congregation could help you and others grow in these practices?
6. Where in this chapter did you sense the Spirit moving in you? Return to that word, sentence, or paragraph and listen for where your heart is being stirred. Bring your feelings, questions, or responses to God in prayer and/or journaling.

7
Responding to the Living Word

In the Word proclaimed—read, preached, and sung—we hear the living Lord addressing us. In the silences preceding and following the gift of the word, extending as long as the mood of the congregation can be stretched to allow, we let this living Word continue to deepen in us, permeating our hearts and taking root in our desires. Where does this Word catch fire in you? What healing is Jesus hoping to accomplish in your heart or memory, what burdens is he inviting you to unload? What love does he desire for your life, what demonic illusions or fears is he casting out from you? How does your world shift or open up in his presence? And to what new realities is he orienting your attention?

Questions like these are not only for those who at times may seem to lead Jesus around on a short leash. They are for every Christian; we are each invited into a personal and potentially transforming relationship with this living Lord. And to refuse to listen to him as he longs to address us cuts us off from the depth and beauty, intimacy and reality into which worship invites us, Sunday after Sunday. Jesus as Word really does reshape reality. He *is* reality, and we are invited to live in this reality now and forever. We will consider the ways worship extends into all the world in the final chapter, in discernment of vocation. But because God's Word, like earth-renewing rains, cannot come to us without nourishing and life-giving effect (Isa. 55:10-11), we are invited to respond in particular ways.

In the hymn of the day, we let the word expand into our heart's song. If, for example, in your prayer with the story of the prodigal son from the previous chapter you have moved from being a resentful and jealous elder brother, afraid of divine displeasure at your feelings about your coworker, to understanding yourself as a soul cherished right *in* these "unacceptable" feelings and *in* your unbearable work situation, softened from all your tormented self-hatred to relax in the arms of mercy, then this hymn will sing itself in you. Your body rising, your voice swelling, tears perhaps even overflowing at the sweetness of divine love even for entangled sinners like you—these are just what the hymn invites. Pour it out, let your heart sing: "There's a wideness in God's mercy," "The King of love my shepherd is," "Softly and tenderly Jesus is calling."

And so he is. Softly and tenderly, passionately and compellingly, Jesus really is calling you, and in the silence and movement following the proclaimed encounter with him you are invited to respond. In the creed we confess this Christian faith, not as a litany of facts but as our entrance into that new reality the Word has opened. *We really are* invited to live in a world created and redeemed by God, its every fiber and tissue and galaxy permeated by the One through whom all things were made, who for us and for our salvation became entirely incarnate among us. This is a very different world than the one our fears and rages create, fueled by the fears and rages of authorities and enemies. In this world of love God creates, the one the Spirit vivifies with irrepressible freshness, the one into which Jesus is inviting the *real* you struggling with your rigid elder-brother heart—here, things look very different than in the old world. Here softness with others, with oneself, with the earth, is a way of life. Here mercy endlessly has the last word, and it is powerful. Here the hungry are fed, the sick healed with grace, victims and oppressors greeted with radical love, the hated embraced. Here, in the world the creed delineates, we too are invited to live in Jesus the living *Logos* ("Word") of all creation who loves all rigid hateful hearts, all bruised and hemorrhaging spirits, all suffocating imprisoned bodies. And so we pray for all the people of God in Christ Jesus, and for all creatures according to their needs. We pray that all may live here in this world of love.

We pray that the church in all the world may experience and embody this astonishing mercy of God, that the world in all its places of suffering may taste and see how good the Lord is, that the sick and hungry and traumatized and imprisoned and dying may know the mercy of the Beloved incarnate in us, and that those for whom our hearts soften may be well and faithfully remembered with all the saints in the heart of God. These intercessions spill out along with those of the church in every time and every place. Let the prayers spring not (or at least not *only*) from pre-printed manuals, however elegantly written, but from the pen and hearts of the prayer leader and the gathered community. Let them expand into plenty of silence, for some prayers rise only with considerable patience, are brought forth only into a generous space. Let the people relax into prayer, for prayer takes time, and those hesitant or broken voices timid in emerging, their mumbling so hard to understand, are precious to God and gifts to us all. These are forms of self-offering: we offer to God those who are dear to us and cast ourselves into the thick of the world so desperately in need of love. One day, later or sooner, we will be the ones prayed for in this same congregation, and what a terrifying mercy that will be. For ultimately we are all cast into the arms of God, borne together with one another.

And in the heart of all the world's need, all our dearest loved ones' need, we hear and receive the gift of Christ's peace. Once again we are immersed in that world God comes to rule in love, this time carrying the hearts that desperately need peace. We have received the living

Word and sung of him with joy; we have confessed the faith that constitutes a new world to live in and prayed that all may come home to love. And now, here, this love—this peace—takes very concrete form not only within us but among us: "The peace of the Lord be with you always." This "you" is *plural!* It is an enactment of peace for *us all,* not only me. This broadens our gaze, making clear that this new world Jesus invites me into is actually intended to include not just attractive, desirable, clean-smelling others but the ordinary or boring or annoying people who fill these pews. This peace of the risen Lord Jesus Christ easing our hearts, releasing us from the world of fear and rage, is for us all. And it is for *each of us.* For this plural-peace is directed not to some vague aggregate but to *each* person knit into this congregation, this body. We act this out as we direct our return greeting of peace first to the presider, and then to the individual, real, beloved persons around us. Each person needs to hear the greeting of Jesus' peace in the flesh, directed to *them,* with a handshake or hug, a personal word or welcome, a smile and warmth. For some people, especially single people and the elderly, this may be the only embrace they experience all week. How we need one another right in the flesh! We need friendly touch, loving touch, as a gift of Jesus Christ incarnate. And so we offer ourselves to one another, giving our warmth and welcome, embracing and exposing ourselves to spontaneous human connection.

This self-offering, this response to the living Word, takes its final ritual form in the offertory itself, as someone from our midst brings our monetary gifts and the treasures of bread and wine up to the altar, to become there the means of our salvation and the world's. With our gifts we ourselves are brought to the altar as well. We are the ones resting there, under the gaze of the presider. With these gifts we truly do place our selves entirely at God's mercy, offering ourselves with no holds barred, letting go into that fiery mercy that longs to receive us. Is that impossibly frightening? Yes. But so is any movement of love. The difference from human love is that in offering ourselves to God we know (or rather, we learn over and over throughout our lives) that the One receiving us is utterly, entirely trustworthy.

What's even more amazing is that our self-offering is preceded by God's own. God is not a tyrant, forcing our submission and lording it over us. God *first* offers God's own self to us in a vulnerability just as naked, just as mortal, as ours. In Jesus, in the infant, in the Crucified One, in the Word we have just received, God is poured out for us, in us, with no holds barred. The One whose very heart itself is offered to us is not dominating at all. God invites our self-offering not from some position of inviolate superiority but from the very same place into which we are similarly invited, namely undefended softness and presence. We don't end up vulnerable *before* God on that altar; we are endlessly vulnerable *with* God there. And this movement into the heart of God is our very redemption itself. With bread and wine, the gifts of earth, with our bodies and bank accounts and relationality and all our lives, we are united with Jesus Christ in his eucharistic journey of death and resurrection. There we are on the altar; here he is on the altar. We are one; we are his.

Prayer practices
Self-offering to others: simplicity and tithing
In responding to the Word, in the fullness of what the Living One evokes in us, we offer our hearts over and over to God and to others. There is no offering of oneself to others in all freedom and love that is not also an offering to God, and vice versa. In suggesting simplicity and tithing (giving ten percent of one's income) as a primary practice of self-offering to others, I don't mean to suggest in any way that confessing our faith, heartfelt intercessory prayer for all those in need, and the practice of peace-making in all places of hard-heartedness or violence are less important. By no means!

But I am choosing to focus on this practice because it's so concrete, so material, so essential to a joyfully this-worldly spirituality like Lutheranism. For it is here that our "prayer-rubber" hits the road.

Perhaps you already live as simply as you can, so as to give as much as possible to those in need. Perhaps you already tithe, or double-tithe, or give even beyond that as a way of living as expansively in the world God loves as you can. If so, you are clearly in the minority in our culture. According to U.S. demographic data, Americans give between two and four percent of their income to charity, with most people falling between two-and-a-half and three percent (www.theatlantic.com/images/issues/200501/2005-01maps.pdf). And those who give the most generously to charity are not the rich but the poor; the percentage of income given to others rises, surprisingly, the *lower* the income bracket. Thus, for most of us, the more we have, the more we think we need and deserve.

Yet we know from scripture that having and hoarding, wealth and the security we think it brings, are diametrically opposed to the way of the God of the desert, of the prophets, and especially of Jesus Christ. These are the ways of fallen humanity, the ways God over and over tries to woo us away from. The way of Jesus Christ is not one of security at all but of radical availability on *every* level of reality to those in need. We know these things, but we find them hard to live out. Horrifying images of famine or disaster, refugees or victims of trauma, may loosen our purse strings in an intense flood of compassion, but we often have little long-term interest in contributing to a systematic worldwide shift of resources from rich (which we surely are) to poor. Once the cameras go away, and the latest disaster is passé, we may return to our usual life without much further thought for global economic injustice, poverty, starvation, or suffering.

Yet God does not forget those who suffer each moment of each day. And here's what's even more surprising, as we try to block our ears against new assaults of compassion fatigue or turn quickly past images of more starving people: those who suffer each moment, the ones God never forgets, include us! The life our wealth creates has constructed walls between persons, families, countries, rich and poor. Modern conveniences often have devastating social implications: long commutes and frantic lifestyles, technology overload and rootless mobility, machine-driven culture and alienation from the earth, the neighbors, one's parents and children and soul and God. What if Jesus were right? What if, in fact, the person who accumulates more and more, building ever bigger barns to hold it all (an image for our culture if there ever was one) really *is* quite simply a "fool" (Luke 12:20)? What if, in fact, the way of simplicity were not only good for those to whom we give the money not spent on electronics and name brands and guzzled gas, but also good for us? Let me not deny that money given to the poor is good for them. People really do need access to clean drinking water, safe housing, antibiotics, sustainable agriculture, education, and so forth. It is safe to wager that the world's providing these things for every single child and adult on earth truly is the will of God. But in the mystery of God it is also true that the sacrifices we rich make to invest in that great and holy desire of God turn out not to be deprivations at all but infinitesimal building blocks toward healing those terrifying alienations from earth, others, and God at the heart of *our* souls! "For where your treasure is, there your heart will be also" (Matt. 6:21). Invite Jesus along next time you buy a car, or a gadget, or a diamond, and see where his heart leads. Chances are your heart will be happier where his is . . . and so will the rest of the world.

Self-offering to God: silent retreat

To many Christians, the practice of retreat seems foreign, something only for "holy" people. Perhaps at work you have "retreats," but they're probably intensive work sessions in a different location. Or perhaps your congregation spends a weekend at the church camp once a year. That's more like what this chapter suggests: providing time in Christian community for relaxation, worship, Bible study, and immersion in creation. Or perhaps your prayer group puts together a weekend intentionally designed for deepening your faith in one way or another. That gets even closer to what I mean by *retreat*, though it may not include sustained silence.

When I speak of retreat, I have in mind several days, or a week or more, spent in silence with God. Retreats or conferences in which people converse between sessions and at meals have tremendous value. But here I want simply to suggest the possibility of silent retreat in which, outside of possible group or individual sessions, people do not converse. As we saw in chapter 5, the practice of silence is at first intimidating for many people. What would I possibly do all day? The answer to that question is the reason this practice is located here, rather than as a practice in the chapter on silence. I am suggesting retreat as a practice specifically of *self-offering to God in response to the Word*. That is, what you do all day is precisely that: in whatever ways the Spirit guides and leads, you respond to the living Word in prayer, offering yourself to God at a level of encounter typically unavailable outside the silent retreat context. You may be surprised to discover the degree of presence available for God when phone, computer, work, family, TV, newspaper, mail, housework, chores, and the hundred daily distractions of your life are absent, not to mention the simple, ordinary social glue of small talk. If you are staying in a retreat center or monastery, it can be a revelation to live in intense mutual companionship with others yet without any necessity to greet, chat, or interact, with everyone's attention directed in some form or another to God. As the retreat continues, the capacity for internal silence deepens and with it the space available for encounter with God who is so eager to meet us. By the time your retreat ends, you may wish you could stay much longer! In fact, you may feel as if you're just arriving with God. And that's the point. The point of retreat is not to stay there forever but to come home with new depths of connection to God, and renewed desire and resources to continue this mutual presence of love in your everyday life.

Retreat formats vary. Many Catholic and Anglican centers or monastic communities welcome silent retreatants and often provide individual spiritual direction or group programs. If you desire a retreat but group or individual direction is not available, you may find other ways to let the Holy Spirit guide you. Your pastor, spiritual director, or experienced friends will surely have ideas if you need them. But on any retreat, don't over-structure yourself. Chances are God doesn't have heroic spiritual athletics in mind. Art work (or play), long walks, more time in prayer, naps, Bible reading, journaling, any of the practices of this book—this is your chance to let the Spirit guide you deeper into the desires you never have time for, the emotion you've been repressing, the heart-stirrings you've been ignoring.

However your retreat is structured (or not!), its sole purpose is giving your heart plenty of grace, time, rest, and nourishment to be entirely present to God in ways the press of ordinary life doesn't usually allow. It's all about mercy: living in the mercy of God at levels of yourself you hardly knew existed, letting that mercy wash over you, flow into you, saturate you, permeate your very bones. And the great joy is that this presence to God in love doesn't end when you return home. What began or deepened or intensified on retreat may well dim a bit once the press of daily life starts up again, but the One you allowed so close will never leave you. All your daily service, the ways you offer yourself to and for and with others at home or in the world, become charged with the sweetness of mercy of God in you, God with you. Far from undermining your service to others and the poor, larding you with self-indulgence, retreat brings you home eager to love God all the more fully throughout your life. And what you discover so amazingly on retreat is just as true at home: the more you can let God love you passionately, endlessly, in all the fullness your body and spirit desire, in all the fullness God constantly longs to pour out in you, the more freely you can love others. It's all about mercy: taste and see.

For reflection, discussion, journaling, or spiritual direction

1. Which parts of the creed are most meaningful to you? Most confusing or difficult? How does confession of faith draw you, personally, into the reality of God?

2. Who writes the intercessory prayers in your congregation? Is time provided for prayers from the community?

3. How do you generally experience the peace in your congregation? What would you miss most if it were left out?

4. How do you personally, or in your family, distinguish between wants and needs? How do you determine the amount you give to church and charity? In your experience, what are the blessings of giving?

5. Have you ever been on a silent retreat? If so, what was that experience like for you? If not, what most attracts you about the possibility of retreat for yourself?

6. Are there ways you sense God inviting you to grow in offering yourself?

7. Where in this chapter did you sense the Spirit moving in you? Return to that word, sentence, or paragraph and listen for where your heart is being stirred. Bring your feelings, questions, or responses to God in prayer and/or journaling.

8
Body of Christ:
Eucharist and Vocation

In holy communion we receive the living Lord in our bodies. The Word becomes flesh. In the Lord's supper the Word we have been hearing, to whom we have been responding, now becomes *visible,* tangible, edible. Here the incarnation of Jesus Christ takes its fullest form as his body and blood permeate ours. Martin Luther never ceased to be amazed at this miracle of our being united to Jesus Christ. For Luther, faith is never merely *belief* in Christ, cognitive assent to him as a mere object of faith. Instead, faith is our *participation* in the living and present reality of Jesus Christ. Faith brings about a real union with Christ fully present in the believer, and this union is intended to be transforming. Luther's highly incarnational theology led him to take seriously our participation in the very reality and life of Jesus Christ to whom we are united by grace through faith. As participants in the "happy exchange" by which Jesus takes on all that is ours and imparts all that is his, including even the essence of divine life, Christians truly partake of that divine life.

Raised within the late-medieval world of prolific venerations, superstitions, and fund-raising methods centering on the mass, a complex symbolic world incorporating every element of Christian and human life, Luther found the Lord's supper at the center of his reform agenda from the outset. But it was the dispute with Ulrich Zwingli, culminating in the Marburg Controversy of 1529, which elicited from Luther his richest thinking to date on the sacrament of the altar. In two eucharistic treatises ("That These Words of Christ, 'This Is My Body,' etc., Still Stand Firm Against the Fanatics" and "Confession Concerning the Lord's Supper") Luther engages the Zwinglians in debate, defending Christ's real presence in the bread and wine against the Zwinglians' more "spiritualizing" view of the sacrament.

Zwingli had challenged traditional notions of the body and blood of Jesus Christ in the sacrament on the grounds that belief in real presence both requires a suspension of rational credulity and violates the dignity of Christ himself, ritually subjecting him to bloody humiliation in the teeth and stomachs of worshipers. Instead, Zwingli defended a "spiritual" understanding of the sacrament, in which one memorializes Christ's death for our salvation and receives its benefits in spirit alone, without the messy and degrading involvement of flesh, blood, mastication, and digestion evoked by the imagery and language of real presence. Zwingli saw Luther's view (and that of Roman Catholicism) as disgustingly literal, materialistic, even carnal.

To Luther, however, these objections demonstrated Zwingli's own impoverished spiritual imagination. For him, from the moment of Jesus' incarnation, God and human flesh are so inextricably interwoven that now there is no such thing as "God" except in and through and containing the full mortal humanity of Jesus Christ. Luther launches into a defense of the utter materiality of this scandalously enfleshed God, this One who meets us deep in the flesh. It was in real human flesh that he was conceived, born of Mary's faith and viscera, held and suckled from warm breasts, and is not this squalling infant flesh the very salvation of the world? It was in real human flesh that

Jesus touched and healed people, washed and fed and raised them to restored fullness of life. It was in real human flesh that he was betrayed and tortured, crucified and pierced for the unending out-pouring of life for all real human sinners. It was this same real human flesh, Jesus bearing the wounds of his passion, that was raised from the dead. And the miracle for Luther is that, just like those who were privileged to know and touch Jesus in first-century Palestine, we too encounter him *in the flesh*, just as real and just as salvific as so many centuries ago:

> Here in the Lord's Supper he wants to be neither born nor seen nor heard nor touched by us but only eaten and drunk, both physically and spiritually. Accordingly, by this eating we obtain just as much and arrive at the same point as they with their bearing, seeing, hearing, etc.; *and he is just as near to us physically as he was to them.* (*Luther's Works* 37:94, emphasis added)

Luther believed the Zwinglians' view obscured the very heart of Christian faith: the incarnation of God in human flesh and God's desire to meet us similarly deep in the flesh. It is for this reason, he argued, that Jesus instituted the sacrament of the altar, so that we would not need to rely on our minds and spirits alone in some abstract realm to grasp the actuality of salvation, but that our hands and mouths may touch, receive, taste, and swallow this living divine reality in the most tangible, personally available form for us. Both mouth and heart, both body and spirit, are needed for us to receive Jesus' body in all the fullness of his reality.

This flesh of Jesus similarly saves and transforms not only what Zwingli terms our "spiritual" selves, our minds and hearts and souls, but our bodily being as well. It is a sacrament *of* body and spirit, and it is a sacrament *for* body and spirit. It makes tangibly clear the prom-ise of Christian salvation for real human bodies. What vivid images Luther uses:

> [The body of Christ] transforms [those who eat] it and gives
> [them] the Spirit. . . . When the body eats it physically, *this food
> digests the body's flesh* and transforms it so that it too becomes
> spiritual, i.e. alive and blessed forever. . . . To give a simple
> illustration of what takes place in this eating: *it is as if a wolf
> devoured a sheep and the sheep were so powerful a food that it
> transformed the wolf and turned it into a sheep.* So, when we eat
> Christ's flesh physically and spiritually, *the food is so power-
> ful that it transforms us into itself.* (*Luther's Works* 37:100–101,
> emphasis added)

For Luther, the flesh of Jesus has profound implications for our whole selves, body and spirit. And far from this divine flesh being degraded by its passage through the human digestive process, just the opposite is true: this flesh "digests" us! Incorporated into our cells and tissues, the flesh of Jesus works its transformative effect from within this most interior permeation of our very being. When we eat him, his body transforms us, via this process of divine metabolism, into his own life incarnate in, with, and under ours. Deep in the flesh, we taste and receive and experience the indwelling divine life of Jesus Christ himself, in all his fullness of crucified and risen humanity, given and poured out for us.

The Zwinglians worried that the glory of Christ was debased by the materiality of the body of Christ for Luther. But for Luther it is precisely this passion of God to enter deep into the very marrow of human bones, tissue of human flesh, depth of human suffering and degradation, that marks the scandal and never-failing wonder of Christianity: this *is* the glory of Christ! Luther's eucharistic writings help move conversation about spirituality to a whole new level, one that includes the whole human being, body and soul, in that transforming union with Christ that saves us. And this points the way to implications for eucharistic practice in our own parishes, so that precisely this juxtaposition, this paradox stretched as far as it possibly can—*God* and *flesh*—can become a source of joy and nourishment to starving people of every kind.

We may at times lose sight of how astonishing an assertion "the Word became flesh" is. In Jesus Christ, *flesh* is the very dwelling-place of God: and both are drawn together for us, in us, in holy communion. The body of Jesus Christ is the meeting place between God, humanity, and creation, and our reception of his body in our bodies invites us into participation in divine life itself. This has powerful implications for worship. For instance, those who suffer depression, shame, or grief often find there are times they simply cannot pray with their heads or even their hearts. They can't focus verbally on concepts, nor sense and feel the love of God emotionally. They experience themselves as numb, shut down, and God as far off. In these dark-night periods, it is crucial that the church provides bodily ways to pray: even if head and heart are numb, people can still receive Jesus' body and blood in their hands, into their own body and blood. And Luther reminds us in that powerful quote about the sheep and the wolf that Jesus' presence is just as transforming and real physically, as it is mentally or emotionally. Luther's understanding invites us to proclaim Christ's eucharistic immersion in us even and especially in our places of pain and sin and suffering. Many wonderful hymns help people sing the connections between Jesus Christ, the sacraments, and their own bodies, feelings, needs, and longings. So eucharist—communion—is practiced, preached, and sung, that the connection between word and sacrament may shine and people may have multiple avenues of access, over and over, to the One who comes in all fullness to them too, deep in *their* flesh.

And ultimately, the bodily presence of our Lord invites us to reflect on how eucharistic practice in this profoundly Lutheran understanding relates to the world, to our political life and resistance to evil. In his own context of devastating evil, Dietrich Bonhoeffer made the connection between the practice of worship and that of risky worldly resistance. Bonhoeffer believed that the practice of paying attention to Jesus' body immersed in us, in whatever forms our bodies and spirits most need, necessarily also opens us into attentiveness to this same body in others, in the poor, in the earth, in the world itself in its ongoing crucifixion.

Bonhoeffer points to the inseparability of worship and political resistance with and for those most in need: where the Crucified One *is,* whether in Nazi Germany or here and now. As at all times in human history, human and creaturely bodies are at risk today: starving refugee bodies in Sudan, bombed bodies in Iraq and the Holy Land, tsunami-wrecked bodies in Asia, battered bodies in homes across the nation, homeless bodies on our streets, addicted bodies, imprisoned bodies, dying bodies in our hospitals, and newborn bodies squalling to life. Our own bodies experience illness and fragility, childbirth and hunger, pleasure and joy and mortality. And our earth's body is tortured as never before in human history, its capacity to sustain human life terribly threatened. Our capacity to attend to the needs of bodies of all kinds, far from removing us from some "spiritual" realm where God lives, instead *is* our opportunity to participate in God's loving and healing work of creation and redemption. And the mystery of vocation—our holy invitation into this never-ending love of God—allows us to live more and more of our lives inside Jesus' eucharistic permeation of all things. Eucharist then becomes not only a Sunday-morning gift but a way of life every day, as our lives participate ever more fully in God's loving and healing transformation. By our attentiveness to Jesus' call, we become increasingly able to invest our very lives in service of God's incarnate tenderness in us, for us, and through us. Thus does our worship take flesh in us, in the world: real prayer, real presence.

Prayer practices
Body care
Eucharistic spirituality both provides and requires deepening sensitivity to the body. Some of us are inundated with body-care. Parents

of young children may feel at times as if they do nothing but change diapers, clean faces and hands, wash clothes, feed hungry mouths, and then change the diapers again. Those who care for the sick, similarly, may feel they have plenty of body-care in their world. But perhaps for these parents and caregivers most of all, the practice of reverent body-care can be grace. If on some level every body we touch participates in the flesh of Jesus himself, then each bath or meal, even the most routine hygiene, becomes a place of reverence. We don't have to exit our normal worlds to find Christ present; here he is, right in the flesh. In touching the bodies entrusted to my care, I touch Jesus. Of course, there is no denying how exhausting and even unpleasant such body-care can be; it's far from glamorous most of the time. We catch a glimpse of why this incarnational religion itself has so often been called disgusting—don't we want to get *away* from the body? And yet in Jesus we discover to our amazement that this is the very work of God: to feed the hungry, to bind up the wounded, to clothe the naked, to wash and embrace the sick, to cherish the needy. Surely our children and the bedridden among us count among those "least of these" in whom Jesus is so intimately welcomed. And for those with the opposite problem of new parents or nursing home aides, namely excessive *dis*connection from human bodies, the eucharistic presence of Jesus Christ can be even more radical. To them this body calls from all directions: in homeless shelters and hospitals, in hospices and day care centers, in soup kitchens and AIDS clinics and refugee camps, the living body of Jesus Christ begs our care. Go meet him. Touch him. Clean him and feed him. Love him.

And let him come close to you as well. Those who care nearly non-stop for others' bodies are often too tired to attend to their own. For them, and for all who experience their own flesh as abhorrent or dirty or ugly, a practice of eucharistic body care can be transforming as well. This is particularly true for those who have suffered abuse, assault, or other forms of trauma, including combat. The experience of trauma causes deep-seated alienation from one's feelings, memories, and core sense of personal identity, all rooted in the traumatized body. Yet bodily participation in Jesus' life draws one's own wounds into healing contact with his and reveals as sacred such wounded flesh permeated by his. A eucharistic spirituality thus allows a victim of violence to begin to perceive his or her body as worthy of attention and care, as itself bearing Jesus' body and presence. Here, caring for one's body and its concrete needs becomes a form of prayer, one's flesh no longer attacked and hated but the place we encounter him whose body and blood saturate the very cells of our being. In a similar way, those who suffer addictions of all kinds—hungers and thirsts that feel nearly unbearable—can learn to experience *right in their very bodies* the One who is the food and drink for which we all long: here already permeating us, and insisting on gentle, reverent care for this fragile physical miracle that is our flesh, his dwelling place on earth. Perhaps our table grace might be a place to begin giving thanks for this reverence of Jesus for our bodies, even as we cherish his as well. What could be more eucharistic—more redolent of thanksgiving—than to bless the Lord for every bite we eat, and learn the ways our bodies are interwoven with his throughout creation?

Discernment of vocation

And now we return full circle to the beginning of the book. We heard there the story of Jesus calling Peter to follow him: a whole new vocation for him. And so it is for us in word and sacrament with the One who makes all things (even us) new. The practices we have been exploring are lived primarily outside of worship, becoming part of the fabric of ourselves as we live ever more attentively to God. But their heart is always in worship, their purpose solely the deepening of our capacity to worship in Spirit and in truth. We pray all week but this does not somehow replace worship. On the contrary, the more we pray, the more eager we are come together with others God seeks and loves, others who long with us to hear the word and share the Lord's supper. In worship these prayer practices find their fulfillment, their purpose, just as one might say that Peter's capacities to see, listen, and speak were developed throughout his life but found their deeper purpose the day Jesus showed up. Peter found himself seeing the Lord, hearing his word, responding to him—just the practices we have been learning here! In worship, we too find Jesus coming to us, and if we are able to welcome him, hear him, respond to him, and follow him, the skills we practice in prayer will be well used.

It is for worship that our prayer practices prepare us. But our worship doesn't end when the liturgy sends us forth. Like Peter, we too are called into new lives of discipleship. And the listening that allows us to hear *our* call in the world is part of the practice called *discernment*.

Peter's call is to "fish for people." But what is *your* call? In what ways is God wanting to call you in new directions small or large? The practice of discernment is the living link between worship and all the rest of our lives. To the extent that we, like Peter, hear and respond faithfully to the One who appears in our lives, climbs into our boats, and changes us completely, we too will leave our nets and live as disciples not only Sunday mornings, but in our vocations, our jobs, our relationships, our homes, our citizenship.

Discernment is a huge subject. It is in a sense the practice of a lifetime, much bigger than we can explore here. Perhaps for now it is enough simply to point to it and invite you into the journey that began for Peter that day on the shore. Peter could never have predicted how God was going to enter his life that day or what new directions would ensue—and neither can you, neither can I. We're blind and deaf and cranky and hard-hearted, *and* God is always full of surprises and almost never does what we expect. So discernment is both difficult and endlessly joyful. Read and learn about discernment, explore it in spiritual direction for your own prayer and life, and don't be afraid. The surest test of an authentic discernment is the feeling of joy and profound, loving connection to God it spontaneously elicits as it touches your heart's deepest desire. This is unmistakable, a different order of experience altogether from vague fantasies or ordinary, half-plodding prayer. The gift of accepting and obeying what is discerned is the invitation to stay in this great joy and the intimacy of God's presence and to live it out in the world, in real life. Such living almost inevitably unfolds into unimagined further gifts for and with others. The pleasure of discernment and all contemplative prayer, of staying close to God all along the way, opens up into our very way of life when we act on discerned vocation. Thus does worship expand to fill our lives, the entire world we inhabit, indeed the cosmos itself. And thus do we follow Jesus in newness of life.

For reflection, discussion, journaling, or spiritual direction

1. What does this chapter's emphasis on Jesus' physical indwelling and transformation mean to you? Is this emphasis new to you, or is it close to what you already experience and believe?

2. What is your favorite dimension of holy communion?

3. Zwingli ridiculed the Lutherans as worshipers of an "edible…baked, roasted, ground-up God" (*Luther's Works* 37:22, note 24). Are there places you struggle with the doctrine or practice of the Lord's supper? What does Jesus' "real presence" mean to you?

4. Do you commune weekly? If not, is that a function of ability, availability, or desire?

5. To what extent do you think the earlier church practice requiring confession before communion was appropriate? Do you practice this in some form yourself? What does it mean to you?

6. Does Jesus' permeation of your body through his body and blood change the way you view your body or other human bodies?

7. How can your daily life reflect greater reverence toward our beleaguered earth in which Jesus is endlessly incarnate?

8. What do you sense you are here on earth for, in God's view?

9. Where in this chapter did you sense the Spirit moving in you? Return to that word, sentence, or paragraph and listen for where your heart is being stirred. Bring your feelings, questions, or responses to God in prayer and/or journaling.

Bibliography

Bass, Dorothy C., ed. *Practicing Our Faith: A Way of Life for a Searching People.* San Francisco: Jossey-Bass, 1997.

Bass, Dorothy C., and Don C. Richter, eds. *Way to Live: Christian Practices for Teens.* Nashville: Upper Room Books, 2002.

Batchelder, David. *All Through the Day, All Through the Year: Family Prayers and Celebrations.* Minneapolis: Augsburg, 2000.

Bonhoeffer, Dietrich. *Discipleship.* Trans. Barbara Green and Reinhard Krauss. *Dietrich Bonhoeffer Works, English Edition (DBWE),* vol. 4. Minneapolis: Fortress Press, 2001.

_____. *Life Together/Prayerbook of the Bible.* Ed. Geffrey B. Kelly. Trans. Daniel W. Bloesch and James H. Burtness. *DBWE* 5. Minneapolis: Fortress Press, 1996.

Casey, Michael. *Sacred Reading: The Ancient Art of Lectio Divina.* Ligouri, MO: Triumph, 1996.

Dahill, Lisa E. "Spirituality in Lutheran Perspective." *Word & World* 18 (Winter 1998): 68-75.

Daily Texts 2005: Bible Verses & Prayers for Each Day of the Year. Alexandria, MN: Mount Carmel Ministries, 2004.

Dawn, Marva. *Keeping the Sabbath Wholly: Ceasing, Resting, Embracing,*

Feasting. Grand Rapids, MI: Eerdmans Publishing Co., 1989.

Farnham, Suzanne G., Stephanie A. Hull and R. Taylor McLean. *Grounded in God: Listening Hearts Discernment for Group Deliberations*. Harrisburg, PA: Morehouse Publishing, 1996.

Farrington, Debra K. *Romancing the Holy: Gateways to Christian Experience*. New York: Crossroad, 1997.

Foster, Richard J. *Celebration of Discipline: The Path to Spiritual Growth*, 3rd edition. San Francisco: Harper San Francisco, 1998.

_____. *Prayer: Finding the Heart's True Home*. San Francisco: Harper San Francisco, 1992.

Gerding, Jeri. *Drawing to God: Art as Prayer, Prayer as Art*. Notre Dame, IN: Sorin Books, 2001.

Green, Thomas H., SJ. *Weeds Among the Wheat: Discernment: Where Prayer and Action Meet*. Notre Dame, IN: Ave Maria Press, 1984.

Hanson, Bradley. *A Graceful Life: Lutheran Spirituality for Today*. Minneapolis: Augsburg Fortress, 2000.

Johnson, Ben Campbell. *Listening for God: Spiritual Directives for Searching Christians*. Mahwah, NJ: Paulist Press, 1997.

Klug, Ron. *How to Keep a Spiritual Journal: A Guide to Journal Keeping for Inner Growth and Personal Discovery*. Minneapolis: Augsburg Fortress, 1993.

Lathrop, Gordon W. *Central Things: Worship in Word and Sacrament*. Minneapolis: Augsburg Fortress, 2005.

Linn, Dennis, et al. *Sleeping with Bread: Holding What Gives You Life*. Mahwah, NJ: Paulist Press, 1994. Family-oriented treatment of the daily examen prayer. Wonderful for use with children.

Luther, Martin. "That These Words of Christ, 'This Is My Body,' Etc., Still Stand Firm Against the Fanatics [1527]," and "Confession Concerning Christ's Supper [1528]," trans. and ed. Robert H. Fischer. *Luther's Works*, vol. 37. Philadelphia: Fortress Press, 1961.

_____. "A Simple Way to Pray [1535]," trans. Carl J. Schindler. *Luther's Works*, vol. 43, ed. Gustav K. Wiencke, 187–211. Philadelphia: Fortress Press, 1968.

Marty, Martin E. *The Lord's Supper.* Expanded edition. Minneapolis: Augsburg, 1997.

McIntosh, Mark A. *Discernment and Truth: The Spirituality and Theology of Knowledge.* New York: Herder & Herder, 2004.

Miller, Charles. *Praying the Eucharist: Reflections on the Eucharistic Experience of God.* Harrisburg, PA: Morehouse, 1995.

Miller, David L. *Friendship with Jesus: A Way to Pray the Gospel of Mark.* Minneapolis: Augsburg Books, 1999. Ignatian contemplation of scripture from a Lutheran perspective.

Morris, Danny E. and Charles M. Olsen. *Discerning God's Will Together: A Spiritual Practice for the Church.* Bethesda, MD: Alban Publications, 1997.

Porpora, Douglas V. *Landscapes of the Soul: The Loss of Moral Meaning in American Life.* Oxford: Oxford University Press, 2001.

Putnam, Robert D. *Bowling Alone: The Collapse and Revival of American Community.* New York: Simon and Schuster, 2000.

Reininger, Gustave, ed. *The Diversity of Centering Prayer.* New York: Continuum, 1999.

Sacred Space: Irish Jesuit daily prayer Web site: http://www.sacredspace.ie/

Sheldrake, Philip. *Befriending Our Desires.* Notre Dame, IN: Ave Maria Press, 1994.

Silf, Margaret. *Going on Retreat: A Beginner's Guide to the Christian Retreat Experience.* Chicago: Loyola Press, 2002.

Stortz, Martha Ellen. *A World According to God: Practices for Putting Faith at the Center of Your Life.* San Francisco: Jossey-Bass, 2004.